Moreton Morre

How to Write a
Marketing Plan

THE SUNDAY TIMES

How to Write a Marketing Plan

John Westwood | Revised Third Edition

KoganPage

LONDON PHILADELPHIA NEW DELHI

This is for Lucinda and Ben
who are forever grateful to their father for his plans

Publisher's note
Every possible effort has been made to ensure that the information contained in this book is accurate at the time of going to press, and the publishers and authors cannot accept responsibility for any errors or omissions, however caused. No responsibility for loss or damage occasioned to any person acting, or refraining from action, as a result of the material in this publication can be accepted by the editor, the publisher or the author.

First published in Great Britain in 1996 by Kogan Page Limited
Second edition 2000
Third edition published in Great Britain and the United States 2006
Revised third edition 2011
Reprinted 2012 (twice)

120 Pentonville Road	1518 Walnut Street, suite 1100	4737/23 Ansari Road
London N1 9JN	Philadelphia PA 19102	Daryaganj
United Kingdom	USA	New Delhi 110002
www.koganpage.com		India

© John Westwood, 1996, 2000, 2006, 2011

The right of John Westwood to be identified as the author of this work has been asserted by him in accordance with the Copyright, Designs and Patents Act 1988.

ISBN   978 0 7494 6150 8
E-ISBN   978 0 7494 6151 5

The views expressed in this book are those of the author, and are not necessarily the same as those of Times Newspapers Ltd.

British Library Cataloguing in Publication Data

A CIP record for this book is available from the British Library.

Library of Congress Cataloging-in-Publication Data

Westwood, John, 1947-
      How to write a marketing plan / John Westwood. -- Rev. 3rd ed.
            p. cm.
      ISBN 978-0-7494-6150-8 -- ISBN 978-0-7494-6151-5   I. Marketing-
Management.   I. Title.
      HF415.13.W48 2010
      658.8'02--dc22

                                                                        2010022256

Typeset by Jean Cussons Typesetting, Diss, Norfolk
Printed and bound in India by Replika Press Pvt Ltd

Contents

Preface

This book is different from most business books. It is a practical workbook that will enable you to prepare your own marketing plan.

In the course of this book, you will follow the development of a marketing plan for a fictitious company – The Equipment Manufacturing Company. Step by step you will be shown how to carry out the different steps in marketing planning. Exercises help you to produce sections of your own marketing plan.

By the time you reach the end of this book, we will have completed our marketing plan and you will have completed yours.

The book can be used in many ways:

- **as an individual study guide;**
- **for group marketing planning exercises;**
- **as a textbook for marketing courses.**

Since the completed plan is included at the end of the book, we include the answers as well as the questions!

1

Introduction

Planning is one of the most important roles of management. A company's corporate or business plan runs the business. A company's marketing plan is a key input to the business plan. It should identify the most promising business opportunities for the company and outline how to penetrate, capture and maintain positions in identified markets. It is a communication tool combining all the elements of the marketing mix in a coordinated action plan. It spells out who will do what, when, where and how, to achieve its ends.

An overall company marketing plan can be made up of a number of smaller marketing plans for individual products or areas. These smaller plans can be prepared as and when the occasion requires.

Most books on marketing planning concentrate on theory. This approach is fine for business academics but makes the whole process too complicated for the average sales manager. The approach in this book is a practical one, including only as much theory as is necessary to understand the planning process. Working your way through this book will broaden your understanding of the principles of marketing planning so that you will be able to carry out the background work necessary to put together any type of marketing plan.

It is, however, becoming more common for sales and marketing personnel to have to put together individual plans for a product or an area very quickly. This book is designed as much to help those people as to provide guidance to marketing personnel putting together an overall marketing plan.

Throughout the book we will follow the fortunes of a company manufacturing filters and valves – The Equipment Manufacturing Company. It will be used in examples and as the basis of a marketing plan. The plan will be for all its products for its home market. To get the best out of this book, you should follow this example and prepare an equivalent marketing plan for a product for your own company as we progress through the steps one by one. By the end of the book, you will have your own marketing plan.

Adopting and following the formal structure of the plan (shown later in this book) will make it easier for you to order your thoughts and the facts logically.

It will be easier for:

- **people reading the plan to follow your arguments and to see how you reached your conclusions;**
- **you to present a professional-looking and complete document from even a relatively small amount of information.**

The Equipment Manufacturing Company is a medium-sized company based in the south of England. Key facts are given opposite:

Company name: The Equipment Manufacturing Company

Annual turnover:	£6m
UK sales:	£2m
Export sales:	£4m
Operating profit:	£1.05m
Number of employees:	65

Main products: Valves and filters

List the same information below for your own company or business unit:

Company name: _____

Annual turnover: _____

UK sales: _____

Export sales: _____

Operating profit: _____

Number of employees: _____

Main products: _____

Before we proceed, we need to cover some basic definitions. So first of all, answer the following questions:

What is selling? _____

_____

_____

_____

What is marketing? _____

_____

_____

_____

What is marketing planning?

_____

_____

_____

Check your answers with the definitions given below.

What is selling?

Selling is a straightforward concept which involves persuading a customer to buy a product. It brings in 'today's orders'. It is, however, only one aspect of the marketing process.

What is marketing?

The dictionary definition of marketing is: 'the provision of goods or services to meet consumers' needs'. In other words, marketing involves finding out what the customer wants and matching a company's products to meet those requirements, and in the process making a profit for the company. Successful marketing involves having the right product available in the right place at the right time and making sure that the customer is aware of the product. It therefore brings in 'tomorrow's orders'.

It is the process that brings together the abilities of the company and the requirements of its customers. Companies have to be flexible in order to achieve this balance in the marketplace. They must be prepared to change products, introduce new products or enter new markets. They must be able to read their customers and the marketplace. This balancing process takes place in the 'marketing environment' which is not controlled by individuals or by companies, is constantly changing and must be monitored continuously.

Marketing therefore involves:

- **the abilities of the company;**
- **the requirements of the customer;**
- **the marketing environment.**

The abilities of the company can be managed by the marketing function. It can control four main elements of a company's operation, which are often referred to as 'the marketing mix', also known as the 'four Ps'. These are four controllable variables that allow a company to come up with a policy that is profitable and satisfies its customers:

- **the product sold (Product);**
- **the pricing policy (Price);**
- **how the product is promoted (Promotion);**
- **methods of distribution (Place).**

'Promotion' and 'place' are concerned with reaching your potential customers in the first place, and 'product' and 'price' will allow you to satisfy the customer's requirements.

Exercise

Below we consider the marketing mix for The Equipment Manufacturing Company for the product line 'Standard Filters'.

Standard filters

- *Pricing:* For this product we have adopted a 'discount policy'. We are offering:
  - discounts for online purchases to encourage the use of our online shop;
  - quantity discounts to encourage larger unit purchases;
  - a discount level for next year based on the level of purchases this year.
- *Promotion:* For this product, we have adopted the following approach:
  - we advertise this product in the technical press;
  - we have a range of product brochures that can be downloaded from our website;
  - we carry out regular mailshots and e-mailshots.
- *Distribution:* This product is sold in the UK through our own sales force and independent distributors. It is also available from our online shop. Overseas it is sold through independent distributors.

Consider the marketing mix for your company's products. For each of your main products write some notes on the pricing policy, how the product is promoted and how the product is distributed.

	Product 1	Product 2	Product 3
Pricing	_____	_____	_____
	_____	_____	_____
	_____	_____	_____
Promotion	_____	_____	_____
	_____	_____	_____
	_____	_____	_____

Distribution   _____   _____   _____

_____   _____   _____

_____   _____   _____

What is marketing planning?

The term *marketing planning* is used to describe the methods of
applying marketing resources to achieve marketing objectives.
This may sound simple, but it is in fact a very complex process.
The resources and the objectives will vary from company to
company and will also change with time. Marketing planning is
used to segment markets, identify market position, forecast
market size, and to plan viable market share within each market
segment.

The process involves:

- **carrying out marketing research within and outside the
  company;**
- **looking at the company's strengths and weaknesses;**
- **making assumptions;**
- **forecasting;**
- **setting marketing objectives;**
- **generating marketing strategies;**
- **defining programmes;**
- **setting budgets;**
- **reviewing the results and revising the objectives,
  strategies or programmes.**

Each of these will be discussed individually in later chapters.

The planning process will:

- **make better use of company resources to identify
  marketing opportunities;**
- **encourage team spirit and company identity;**

- **help the company to move towards achieving its corporate goals.**

In addition, the marketing research carried out as part of the planning process will provide a solid base of information for present and future projects.

Marketing planning is an iterative process and the plan will be reviewed and updated as it is implemented.

Stages in the preparation of a marketing plan

The stages in the preparation of a marketing plan are shown in Figure 1.1.

Set corporate objectives

Corporate objectives are set by top management and this may not be in your brief. Even so, you must be aware of your company's corporate objectives and the ultimate plan should be in line with them.

Carry out external marketing research

Since companies exist and operate in the marketing environment, the first step in a marketing plan is research into that environment. Research is carried out into the markets themselves and then the information collected is analysed in the context of the marketing of the products.

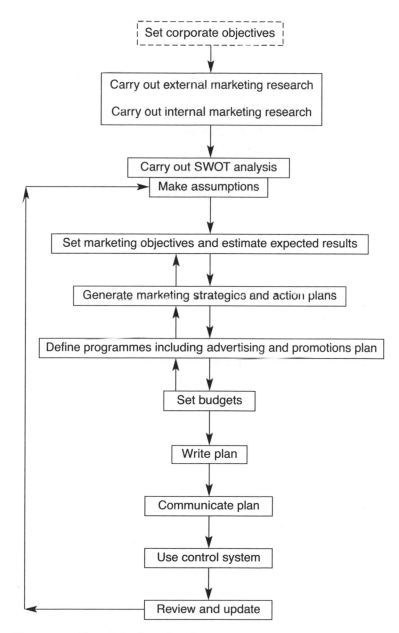

Figure 1.1   The marketing planning process

Carry out internal marketing research

Perhaps even more important than general market information is historical information available 'in house'. This will be sales/order and margin/profit data relating to the products and areas for the plan. This information needs to be put into context in the form of market shares by geographical area and industry type for individual products and in total.

Carry out SWOT analysis

When all the information and opinions have been collected by market research, the materials need to be analysed and presented in a way that will help to make the best decisions. This can be done by selecting the key information and carrying out a SWOT analysis. The method of carrying out SWOT analysis is explained in detail in Chapter 2.

Make assumptions

The plan itself is based on a clearly understood set of assumptions. These relate to external economic factors as well as technological and competitive factors.

Set marketing objectives and estimate expected results

The next step is the key to the whole marketing process: the setting of marketing objectives. This is what you want to achieve – the fundamental aims of the plan. How to set objectives is covered in Chapter 3.

Generate marketing strategies and action plans

Marketing strategies are the methods that will enable you to achieve your marketing objectives. They relate to the elements of the marketing mix – product, price, promotion and place. For each objective, strategies need to be developed relating to these individual elements. First the marketing strategy needs to be set out and then action plans are prepared. This is also covered in Chapter 3.

Define programmes including advertising and promotions plans

Defining programmes means defining who does what, when, where and how.

Set budgets

Objectives can be set and strategies and action plans devised, but they need to be cost-effective. The setting of budgets defines the resources required to carry out the plan and quantifies the cost and also the financial risks involved. It is explained in Chapter 4.

Write plan

Once all the above steps have been carried out you will be in a position to prepare the written plan. The written plan should only contain the key information that needs to be communicated.

Communicate plan

If a plan is not properly communicated to those who will be implementing it, it will fail.

Review and update

Conditions and situations will change and the plan should be regularly reviewed in the light of changing circumstances.

Summary

Marketing planning involves the application of marketing resources to achieve marketing objectives. It is used to:

- **segment markets;**
- **identify market position;**
- **forecast market size;**
- **plan viable market share within each market segment.**

A marketing plan is a document that formulates a plan for marketing products and/or services. A company marketing plan sets out the company's marketing objectives and suggests strategies to achieve them. There is a fixed procedure for carrying out the marketing planning process to enable you to prepare a marketing plan, and the planning process is an iterative procedure.

2

Situation analysis – the marketing audit

The marketing audit is a detailed examination of the company's marketing environment, specific marketing activities and its internal marketing system. In this chapter we will concentrate on the audit of the marketing environment. We will come back in more detail to the marketing mix and the marketing system in later chapters.

The audit of the marketing environment

This is an examination of the company's markets, customers, competitors and the overall economic and political environment. It involves marketing research and the collecting of historical data about your company and its products. It is an iterative process. It is only when you start to analyse your own in-house data that you realise which market sectors you need to look at outside and once you look at the external data you may notice applications that are small for your company, but larger in a market context and therefore require further investigation.

The audit of marketing activity

This is a study of the company's marketing mix – product, price, promotion and place.

The audit of the marketing system

This involves looking at the current structure of the marketing organisation together with its systems.

The marketing environment – market research

At the same time that you consider historical sales data for your company, you need to collect information that will allow it to be put into perspective. This involves market research – collecting information about your markets and then analysing it in the context of the marketing of the products.

Market research is used to:

- **give a description of the market;**
- **monitor how the market changes;**
- **decide on actions to be taken by a company and evaluate the results of these actions.**

Market research data consists of primary data and secondary data. Primary data is data obtained from primary sources, ie directly in the marketplace. This is gathered either by carrying out field research directly yourself or by commissioning a consultant or market research company to carry out the fieldwork for you. Secondary data is not obtained directly from fieldwork, and market research based on secondary data sources is referred to as desk research.

Desk research involves the collection of data from existing sources.

Before looking at other sources, it is usual to start desk research on the internet. A huge amount of information is available online and much of this can be obtained free of charge. Use internet search engines, such as Google (www.google.com), to carry out web searches.

If you want information on milk production, just type in 'milk production' or 'dairy production'. This will get you sites with both data on how to produce milk and sites giving statistical data. So you need to refine your search. Perhaps try 'milk production statistics'. Similarly, if you are really only interested in milk production in Europe or just the United Kingdom, just type in 'milk production + Europe' or 'milk production + UK'.

You can find out a lot about your main competitors by checking out their websites. The 'who are we?' section will often give a potted history of their company and from the 'products' section you will be able to download pdf files of their brochures and datasheets.

Once you have done as much as you can by general web searches, try other sources to get more specific data. These sources could include:

- **Government statistics (from the Office for National Statistics, www.statistics.gov.uk);**
- **market reports and country reports for export markets (UK Trade & Investment, www.uktradeinvest.gov.uk);**
- **company information (from Companies House, www. companieshouse.gov.uk, or companies such as Kompass, www.kompass.co.uk, or Kelly's, www. kellysearch.com);**

- trade directories;
- trade associations (find details of trade associations for your industry from Trade Association Forum, www.taforum.org);
- ready-made reports (from companies such as Keynote, www.keynote.co.uk; Euromonitor, www.euromonitor.com; Mintel, www.mintel.co.uk; and Frost & Sullivan, www.frost.com);
- the internet (industry-specific websites such as www.sugarinfo.co.uk for the sugar industry; www.lfra.co.uk for the food industry; and www.poyry.com for the pulp and paper industry).

The market research information for your marketing plan will consist of *market information* and *product information*.

Market information

Market information needs to tell us:

- *The market's size:*   How big is it?
  How is it segmented/ structured?
- *Its characteristics:*   Who are the main customers?
  Who are the main suppliers?
  What are the main products sold?
- *The state of the market:*   Is it a new market?
  A mature market?
  A saturated market?
- *How well are companies doing?*   Relative to the market as a whole?
  In relation to each other?
- *Channels of distribution:*   What are they?

- *Methods of communication:*   What methods are used – press, TV, internet, e-mail, direct mail?
  What types of sales promotion?
- *Financial:*   Are there problems caused by: Taxes/duties?
  Import restrictions?
- *Legal:*   Patent situation:
  Product standards
  Legislation relating to agents
  Trademarks/copyright
  Protection of intellectual property (designs software, etc)
- *Developments:*   What new areas of the market are developing?
  What new products are developing?
  Is new legislation or new regulations likely?

Product information

Product information relates to your own company, your competitors and the customers:

- *Potential customers:*   Who are they?
  Where are they located?
  Who are the market leaders?
  Do they own competitors?
- *Your own company:*   Do existing products meet customers' needs?
  Is product development necessary?

Are completely new products required?
What would be the potential of a new product?
How is your company perceived in the market?

- *Your competitors:*   Who are they?
How do they compare with your company in size?
Where are they located?
Do they operate in the same market sectors as you?
What products do they manufacture/sell?
How does their pricing compare with your own?
What sales/distribution channels do they use?
Have they recently introduced new products?

Practical example

The Equipment Manufacturing Company sets about carrying out external market research. It is looking for information on valves and filters and companies that manufacture them. For this particular marketing plan it is concentrating on the UK market.

It already has a lot of information on valves. The company belongs to the British Valve & Actuator Association (BVAA). The BVAA produces company profiles of all the valve manufacturers in the UK that belong to the Association, together with details of the types of valves that they produce. Our company manufactures ball valves and from the BVAA website we can see that there are six other manufacturers of ball valves in the BVAA. Other companies manufacture other types of valves – diaphragm, gate, butterfly, etc.

Then they check all of their main competitors' websites. These include www.biggsvalves.com and www.sparcovalves.com for their main UK competitors, and www.texasvalves.com and www.dvk.com for their main overseas competitors. They also check out www.dvk.co.uk, which is the UK website of their German competitor DVK. From these websites they are able to download their competitors' mission statements, product literature and information about new products and other developments, such as the establishment of a new distribution centre by DVK.

Next they go to Companies House (www.companieshouse.gov.uk) and use the WebCHeck service to find information including annual reports for their UK competitors. They are able to purchase the reports online and download them as pdf files. The information given varies – small companies do not have to give turnover and divisions of larger companies may have individual reports. Nevertheless a considerable number of companies still show an annual sales split between UK sales and Export sales.

The next source is the Office for National Statistics, www.statistics.gov.uk, which produces Prodcom statistics. These are details of the value of production, imports and exports of products for the UK. It uses the Prodcom headings set by Eurostat. The information is normally produced in the form of annual data publications. They type 'valves' into the search engine on the website and it brings up a number of reports. The reports are on 'Product Sales and Trade: Taps and Valves', so they have to separate out the information relating to ball valves. By subtracting imports from exports, and taking this figure from UK production, they are able to establish that the UK market for ball valves is £10 million; they sell £1 million in the UK market. Prodcom statistics also tell them that imports are £4 million, of which £2 million comes from other EU countries.

Finally, the BVAA advises them that there are a number of published reports by companies like Frost & Sullivan (www.frost.com) and small market research companies. They are able to obtain a number of reports including *Pumps and Valves in the Water Industry*, and *A Survey of Equipment Suppliers to the Food Industry*.

They have now been able to establish that the UK market for their product is about £10 million; they have sales of £1 million. Imports are £4 million, of which £2 million comes from the EU. From this data they can produce a table showing UK market shares (see Table 2.1).

Table 2.1   Market share information

UK MARKET SHARE – BALL VALVES

Company	£000	%
Equipment Mfg	1,000	10
Biggs Valves	2,200	22
Sparco Valves	800	8
DVK (German)	1,600	16
Texas Valves (USA)	800	8
Others	3,600	36
Total	10,000	100

Exercise

Now consider the product(s) and area(s) that you will use for your marketing plan. Follow through the same exercise that we have just carried out for The Equipment Manufacturing Company. Start by using the internet to track down information relating to your market and your competitors. Do you have a trade association? If so, contact them and see what information they have. Also contact your local Chamber of Commerce. Put together as much information as you can on the products, the markets, competition, market shares, etc.

Internal market research

In addition to the external market research, your company has a wealth of data that is invaluable in the preparation of a marketing plan. In fact the problem is more likely to be that there is too much data so that you cannot easily see which information is the most important. It is likely that much data will not be available in the right form. You may have overall sales data, but not data itemised for individual product lines or market segments.

The historical data relevant to the preparation of your marketing plan is basically sales/order data separated and analysed in such a way that it reflects the key market segments into which you sell your products.

What is market segmentation?

Different customers have different needs. They do not all require the same product and they do not all require the same product benefits. Even with an individual product, not all customers will buy it for the same reasons. Market segmentation allows you to consider the markets you are actually in and the markets that your company should be in.

You need to be able to split your customer base up into groups of customers who all have similar needs. Each of these groups constitutes a market segment.

For consumer goods and services, it is usual to classify the end-users by the use of methods of classification which separate consumers by socio-economic group, age, sex, occupation or region.

The marketing of industrial goods is different to services. Because the customer is usually another company or a government department, the number of customers is more likely to be ten thousand than ten million and could be only a few hundred in the case of suppliers to power stations, coal mines, etc.

The main ways of defining segments here are by:

- **geographical area;**
- **industry or industry subsector;**
- **product;**
- **application;**
- **size of end-user;**
- **distribution channel – distributor, equipment manufacturer, end-user.**

Segmentation can also be based on:

- **order size;**
- **order frequency;**
- **type of decision-maker.**

The key to market segmentation is to let the marketplace segment itself, because the individual segments exist independently of the company and its products.

For the products and markets covered by your plan, you

should collect and present information going back two or three full years together with this year's historical sales. You should show margin information relating to those sales, where it is available. You should also adjust figures for inflation and have them available in their actual and adjusted forms.

Information checklist

It is useful to prepare an information checklist for a marketing plan before you start to collect data. The exact content will vary, depending on the scope of your plan, but it should include details of the segmentation that you want for sales, the split of your customer base, and competitor activity/market shares. The detail of the information will vary depending on the type of company, and this will mean that details listed in the checklist will also vary and should be customised to your company.

In order to prepare a marketing plan for the UK market for all its products The Equipment Manufacturing Company has put together a checklist of information required shown below.

1. Sales history

The last three years' sales by value (including margins where available) for:

- sales areas: South, Midlands, North, Wales, Scotland/NI;
- product groups: ball valves, type 'S', type 'A' and type 'K' filters, packages;
- main equipment and spares.

Also unit sales:
- number of valves by model size;
- number of filters by model size.

2.   Customers

Total number of customers by:

- sales area: South, Midlands, North, Wales, Scotland/NI;
- products bought: ball valves, type 'S', type 'A' and type 'K' filters, packages;
- market: chemical/petrochemical, water treatment, paper, food;
- key customers, ie top 40 by sales turnover.

3.   Competition?

- Who are the competitors for each product group?
- What are the market shares for each product for each competitor?

Now prepare an information checklist for your own company for the products and areas to be covered by your plan.

Information Checklist

1.   Sales history
Prepare last three years' sales by:

- _____
- _____
- _____

2.   Customers
Segment customers by:

- _____
- _____
- _____

3. Competition

How do we want to present competitor information?

- _____
- _____
- _____

How to present the figures

Depending on the scope of the plan, the sales data may be split up into separate tables geographically, by product, by industry or under all of these categories.

The figures can easily be prepared on computer spreadsheets such as Microsoft's Excel or Lotus SmartSuite's Lotus 1-2-3. These programs have the facility for the data entered into the spreadsheet tables to be displayed graphically as well. It is usual when producing tables of historical data on a spreadsheet to extend the form layout to include columns for the years which the marketing plan will cover. The columns for future years will remain blank at this time as the current task is to record historical and current sales data, but it makes it easier later on to project sales figures so that comparisons can be made and trends can be seen.

Table 2.2 shows how the figures could be presented for The Equipment Manufacturing Company for use in their UK marketing plan.

Table 2.2   Sales figures UK (all products)

THE EQUIPMENT MANUFACTURING COMPANY SALES FIGURES					
Sales Area: UK					
	← Actual →			← Forecast →	
Year (all values in £k)	20X3 20X4 20X5			20X6 20X7 20X8	

	20X3	20X4	20X5	20X6	20X7	20X8
Filters	200	450	600			
Valves	1,400	1,200	1,000			
Components	300	350	400			
Total	1,900	2,000	2,000			

Inflation over the past three years has been 3 per cent per year. This information therefore needs to be adjusted for inflation (Table 2.3).

Table 2.3   Sales figures UK (adjusted for inflation)

THE EQUIPMENT MANUFACTURING COMPANY SALES FIGURES						
Sales Area: UK						

	20X3	20X4	20X5	20X6	20X7	20X8
Filters	200	437	566			
Valves	1,400	1,165	943			
Components	300	340	377			
Total	1,900	1,942	1,886			

Another way to look at volume growth is to analyse unit sales rather than sales value (Table 2.4).

Table 2.4   Unit sales of filters

THE EQUIPMENT MANUFACTURING COMPANY SALES

Sales Area: UK
Product: Filters

	← Actual →			← Forecast →		
Year (number of units)	20X3	20X4	20X5	20X6	20X7	20X8
Type S	402	396	412			
Type A	100	120	140			
Type K	50	100	150			
Packages	4	8	14			
Total	556	624	716			

The profitability of sales is very important. It is therefore necessary also to show the margins being made on the sale of different products (Table 2.5).

Table 2.5   Sales figures for the UK including margin information

THE EQUIPMENT MANUFACTURING COMPANY SALES FIGURES

Sales Area: UK

Year	20X3		20X4		20X5		
	Sales	Gross profit	Sales	Gross profit	Sales	Gross profit	Comments
	£k	%	£k	%	£k	%	
Filters	200	40	450	40	600	40	
Valves	1,400	30	1,200	30	1,000	30	
Components	300	60	350	60	400	60	
Total	1,900	35.8	2,000	37.5	2,000	39	

More detailed information should also be shown for the main geographical areas of the plan (Table 2.6).

Table 2.6   Sales figures for valves in the UK

SALES FIGURES					
Sales Area:	UK				
Product:	Valves				
	◄――― Actual ―――►			◄――― Forecast ―――►		
Year (all values in £k)	20X3	20X4	20X5	20X6	20X7	20X8
South	295	250	230			
Midlands	485	415	360			
North	525	420	300			
Wales	45	55	60			
Scotland/NI	50	60	50			
Total	1,400	1,200	1,000			

This information could also be shown graphically as in Figures 2.1 and 2.2.

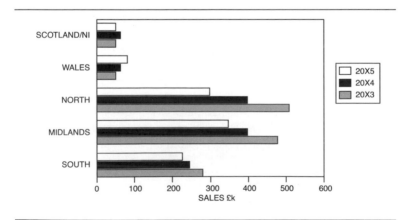

Figure 2.1   Sales figures for valves in the UK

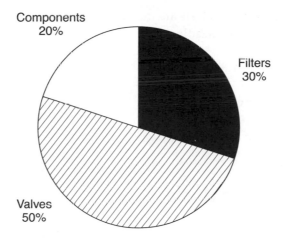

Figure 2.2   UK sales by product

Now prepare a similar set of data for your product for your own example plan. It is important that you carry out the exercise even if you do not have all the data available to complete all of the tables.

Situation analysis

Completing the market research and collecting the historical data about your company and its products is only the first step. You need to analyse this information and present it in a way that can be used for planning. Situation analysis is a process which helps you do this. It:

- **reviews the economic and business climate;**
- **considers where the company stands in its strategic markets and key sales areas;**
- **looks at the strengths and weaknesses of the company – its organisation, its performance and its key products;**
- **compares the company with its competitors;**
- **identifies opportunities and threats.**

The results of this analysis are included in the marketing plan under the following headings:

- **Assumptions;**
- **Sales;**
- **Strategic or key markets;**
- **Key products;**
- **Key sales areas.**

SWOT analysis

The key process used in situation analysis is SWOT analysis. SWOT stands for:

Strengths and Weaknesses as they relate to our Opportunities and Threats in the marketplace.

The strengths and weaknesses refer to the company and its products whereas the opportunities and threats are usually taken to be external factors over which your company has no control. SWOT analysis involves understanding and analysing your strengths and weaknesses and identifying threats to your business as well as opportunities in the marketplace. You can then attempt to exploit your strengths, overcome your weaknesses, grasp your opportunities and defend yourself against threats. This is one of the most important parts of the planning process. SWOT analysis asks the questions that will enable you to decide whether your company and the product will really be able to fulfil your plan and what the constraints will be.

In carrying out SWOT analysis it is usual to list the strengths, weaknesses, opportunities and threats on the same page. This is done by segmenting the page into four squares and entering strengths and weaknesses in the top squares and opportunities and threats in the bottom squares, as shown in Figure 2.3.

The number of individual SWOTs will depend on the scope of

your plan. First you should carry out a SWOT on your company and its organisation. You should also do the same for your main competitors and for your products, geographical areas and market segments covered by the plan.

STRENGTHS	WEAKNESSES
OPPORTUNITIES	THREATS

Figure 2.3   Presentation of SWOT analysis

Exercise

The following figures show a number of SWOT analyses that The Equipment Manufacturing Company has prepared and will use in its UK marketing plan.

Figures 2.4, 2.5, 2.6, 2.7, 2.8 and 2.9 show SWOTs on the company, its sales organisation, a product, a sales area, a market segment and a competitor.

STRENGTHS	WEAKNESSES
■ Part of large UK Group ■ Good image – quality company ■ Good resources – financial, technical ■ Established export sales	■ Sales in UK are not growing ■ Thought of as 'old fashioned' ■ Few marketing staff ■ Website needs updating and expanding
OPPORTUNITIES	THREATS
■ Parent company is investing in new marketing department ■ New Group R&D facility ■ To develop new products ■ To open low-cost factory in Asia	■ Low-priced products from the Far East ■ Niche products from other EU countries

Figure 2.4   Company SWOT analysis

STRENGTHS	WEAKNESSES
■ Large field sales force in UK ■ Have industry specialists ■ New modern offices	■ Many new staff – need experience ■ Staff training required
OPPORTUNITIES	THREATS
■ To recruit new sales manager ■ To restructure sales force ■ To carry out advanced sales training	■ No in-house successor to sales & marketing director ■ Competitors expanding field sales forces

Figure 2.5   Sales organisation SWOT analysis

STRENGTHS	WEAKNESSES
■ Good range of sizes ■ Quality product ■ Solidly built	■ Limited range of materials ■ Heavier than competitors' products ■ High cost/high price
OPPORTUNITIES	THREATS
■ Source product from China ■ Develop new product	■ Cheap imports from Asia ■ Competing products in plastic materials

Figure 2.6 SWOT analysis for product – ball valves

STRENGTHS	WEAKNESSES
■ Large industrial base ■ Industrial sites concentrated in a few areas	■ Many old plants ■ Not many new projects ■ All major competitors present
OPPORTUNITIES	THREATS
■ Refurbish old plants ■ Diversify into new industries, eg water treatment	■ Biggs' strongest area ■ More companies are moving production abroad ■ More companies may shut for good

Figure 2.7 SWOT analysis for a geographical sales area – the North of England

STRENGTHS	WEAKNESSES
■ Strong with filters ■ We have an industry expert	■ A 'lowest price' market ■ Weak with valves ■ No economies of scale
OPPORTUNITIES	THREATS
■ New investment programme to meet EU directives ■ New products, eg motorised timer valve	■ No longer 'buy British' bias ■ Some water companies now owned by foreign companies (French/German/US) ■ Some competitors can package products together ■ Water company owned competitors

Figure 2.8   SWOT analysis for a market segment – Water Industry

THEIR STRENGTHS	THEIR WEAKNESSES
■ Large company ■ Wide product range ■ Relatively high market share ■ Good name	■ Just sacked distributor ■ Inexperienced own sales force ■ Lack service support ■ Old fashioned product
OPPORTUNITIES FOR US	THREATS TO US
■ Ball valves are manufactured in a high-cost factory in Germany ■ New product developments	■ They may set up a service support organisation ■ They are building a low-cost factory in China

Figure 2.9   SWOT analysis for a competitor – DVK (Germany)

Now consider your own sample plan and carry out SWOTs in the same format for:

- your company;
- your sales organisation;
- each of your key products;
- each of your key sales areas;
- each of your key market segments;
- each of your major competitors.

STRENGTHS	WEAKNESSES
OPPORTUNITIES	THREATS

With the completion of the situation analysis we are now ready to move on to setting objectives and deciding strategies.

Summary

At the same time as you consider historical sales data for your company, you need to collect information that will allow it to be put into perspective. This involves market research – collecting information about your markets and then analysing it in the context of the marketing of the products. Depending on the scope of the plan, the sales data may be split up into separate tables geographically, by product, by industry or under all of these categories. Completing the market research and collecting the historical data about your company and its products is only the first step. You need to analyse this information and present it in a way that can be used for planning. Situation analysis is a process which helps you to do this.

3

Objectives, strategies and action plans

Now that we have identified our key strengths and weaknesses, the opportunities and threats to our business, and made assumptions about outside factors that may affect our business, we are in a position to set our marketing objectives. This is the key step in the whole process of preparing a marketing plan.

What is a marketing objective?

Objectives are what we want to achieve; strategies are how we get there. A marketing objective concerns the balance between products and their markets. It relates to *which products* we want to sell into *which markets*. The means of achieving these objectives, using price, promotion and distribution are marketing strategies. At the next level down there will be personnel objectives and personnel strategies, advertising objectives and advertising strategies, etc. There will then be tactics, action plans and budgets – all to enable us to achieve our objectives.

Marketing objectives relate to any of the following:

- **selling existing products into existing markets;**
- **selling existing products into new markets;**
- **selling new products into existing markets;**
- **selling new products into new markets.**

Marketing objectives must be definable and quantifiable so that there is an achievable target to aim towards. They should be defined in such a way that, when your marketing plan is implemented, actual performance can be compared with the objective. They should be expressed in terms of values or market shares, and vague terms such as increase, improve or maximise should not be used.

The following are examples of marketing objectives:

- **to increase sales of the product in the UK by 10 per cent per annum in real terms, each year for the next three years;**
- **to increase sales of the product worldwide by 30 per cent in real terms within five years;**
- **to increase market share for the product in the United States from 10 per cent to 15 per cent over two years.**

Below are listed some preliminary objectives of The Equipment Manufacturing Company:

- **to increase UK sales by 10 per cent per year in real terms for the next three years;**
- **to double ball valve sales to the water industry within three years;**
- **to increase sales of packages to 50 units within three years;**
- **to double market share for filters in the water industry by 20X8;**
- **to double distributor sales in Scotland and NI by 20X8;**
- **to increase overall gross margins from 39 per cent to 43 per cent by 20X8.**

Exercise

Now make a preliminary list of some marketing objectives that you think would be sensible for your sample plan.

In all plans, marketing objectives for the following should be set:

- **sales turnover for the period of the plan by product and market segment;**
- **gross profit on sales;**
- **market share for the period of the plan by product and market segment, where possible.**

The product portfolio

Since marketing objectives relate to *products* and *markets* it is important to understand your present position with regard to both before setting the objectives of your marketing plan.

The growth and decline of all products follows a life cycle curve which can be represented as in Figure 3.1.

Ideally your company will have a portfolio of products, all at different stages in their life cycle, so that balanced growth can be achieved and risks minimised. Figure 3.2 shows a typical product portfolio.

Figures 3.3 and 3.4 show product portfolio curves for the main products manufactured by The Equipment Manufacturing Company.

The 'type S' filters have reached the 'saturation' stage of their life cycle, 'type A' filters are at the 'mature' stage of development and 'type K' filters and packages are at the 'rapid' stage of growth.

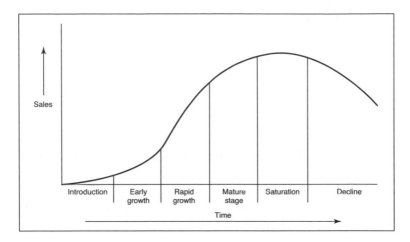

Figure 3.1   Product life cycle curve

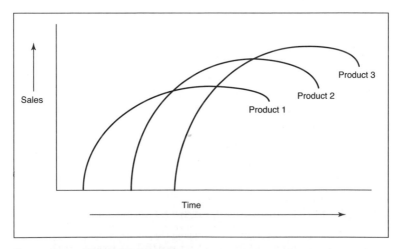

Figure 3.2   A product portfolio

Ball valves are a problem, since they are already in the stage
of 'decline'. Products at this stage of their development will start
to decline even more quickly unless something is done. The
long-term requirement would be to develop a new product, but it

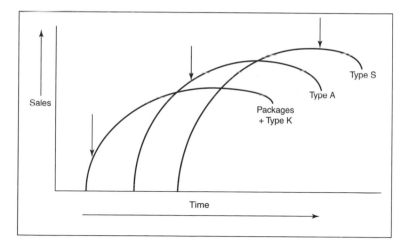

Figure 3.3 Product portfolio for The Equipment Manufacturing Company for filters

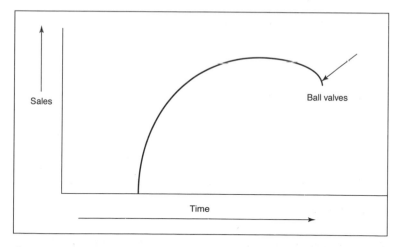

Figure 3.4 Product portfolio for The Equipment Manufacturing Company for ball valves

is often possible to give a product a new, albeit short, lease of life. In the case of The Equipment Manufacturing Company, this is perhaps possible by combining the ball valves with filters in packages for the water treatment industry.

Exercise

Now construct life cycle/product portfolio curves (Figure 3.5) for your company's products and indicate where they are currently on these curves.

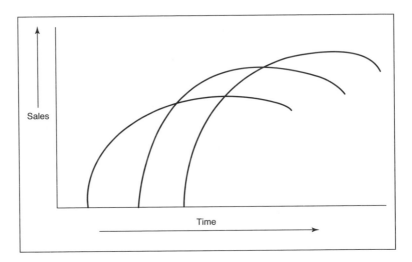

Figure 3.5   Product portfolio exercise

Relative market growth rate and share

In any market the price levels of the major players tend to be broadly similar. In a stable market the price levels of the major players will gradually move together. This does not mean that all these companies will make the same level of profit. If one company has a very large market share, it will benefit from economies of scale and will have lower costs. The company with the highest market share is likely to have the highest profit margin. It is therefore more able to withstand a price war. Its market share also indicates its ability to generate cash. Market share is therefore very important and it should be your aim to achieve market dominance wherever possible.

Cash flow is the most important factor in considering your product portfolio, and your company's ability to generate cash will be dependent, to a large extent, on the degree of market dominance that you have over your competitors.

Some years ago the Boston Consulting Group developed a matrix for classifying a portfolio of products based on relative market shares and relative market growth rates. The 'Boston Matrix' is now widely used by companies to consider their product portfolio.

The products are colourfully described as:

STARS – high market share/high market growth (cash neutral);
CASH COWS – high market share/low market growth (cash generation);
QUESTION MARKS – low market share/high market growth (cash drain);
DOGS – low market share/low market growth (cash neutral).

Relative market share is the ratio of your market share to the market share of your biggest competitor. It indicates the level of market dominance that you have over your competitors.

Market growth rate is important for two reasons. In a fast-growing market the sales of a product can grow more quickly than in a slow-growing or stable market. In increasing sales, the product will absorb a high level of cash to support increasing advertising, sales coverage, sales support and possibly even investment in additional plant and machinery. For the purposes of marketing planning, high market growth is normally taken as 10 per cent per annum or more.

The products are entered into the quadrants of the matrix as shown in Figure 3.6.

Question marks can be either newly launched products which have not yet fulfilled expectation, or products that are declining and need further evaluation as to their long-term viability.

Dogs have low market share and are generally unprofitable. These products would be considered as those that could be dropped from the product portfolio.

Stars have a high cost in spending on marketing and research and development, but also contribute considerably to profits. They are broadly speaking neutral from the point of view of cash generation.

Cash cows are mature products with a high market share, but low market growth. They generate high profits and require only a small amount of marketing investment and no research and development spending to keep them where they are.

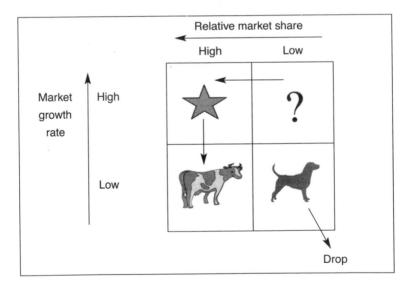

Figure 3.6   Ideal product development sequence

Exercise

Figure 3.7 shows the current position of the product portfolio of The Equipment Manufacturing Company.

The 'type S' filters and 'ball valves' are both cash cows, but ball valves are declining in both relative market share and becoming less and less profitable. 'Packages' are question marks, but will become stars if they continue to grow in relative market share as the market for them expands. 'Type A' and 'type K' filters are both moving into the star sector, with 'type A' a little ahead of 'type K'.

Do similar calculations for the products in your product portfolio and mark them on the matrix in Figure 3.8.

Setting objectives for a marketing plan is not an easy task. Figures for sales turnover or market share cannot just be selected at random. It is an iterative process whereby objectives are set, strategies and action plans are

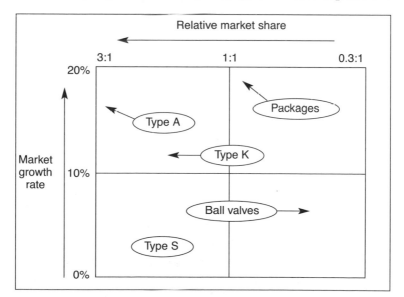

Figure 3.7   Portfolio matrix of The Equipment Manufacturing Company

developed, and then it is decided whether the planned objectives are impossible, achievable or easy. The objectives are then reappraised and should they be changed, the strategies and action plans would also need to be re-examined.

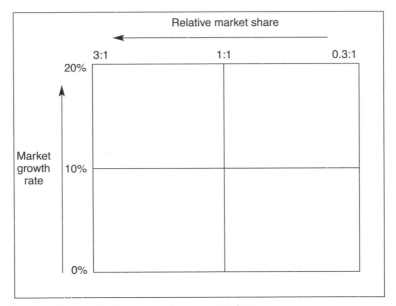

Figure 3.8   Portfolio matrix for your products

At the start of this chapter we set some preliminary objectives for The Equipment Manufacturing Company for their UK plan. The main objective stated with regard to growth was to increase UK sales by 10 per cent per year for the next three years. Is it a sensible objective? In view of the lack of any growth at all in the last three years it is ambitious. It is more likely to be achievable than 20 per cent growth per year. It takes time for new strategies and plans to work. Most marketing plans therefore show more growth in years two and three than in the first year.

We can use gap analysis to decide how realistic our objectives are.

Gap analysis

Gap analysis is a technique with many uses. From the point of view of setting marketing objectives it can be used to help you analyse and close the gap between what your company needs to achieve and what is likely to be achieved if policies are unchanged.

Figure 3.9 shows the original and required sales forecast for a company with the gap to be bridged.

For The Equipment Manufacturing Company the figures for the last three years show no growth at all in the UK market. In our assumptions, we estimate that inflation will be running at 3 per cent in 20X6, 4 per cent in 20X7 and 4 per cent in 20X8. Real growth of 10 per cent per year will therefore produce a 'gap' of £937,000 between the required and originally projected growth. (This figure is based on £2 million × 1.13 × 1.14 × 1.14.) The sales projection for The Equipment Manufacturing Company for the UK plan is shown in Table 3.1.

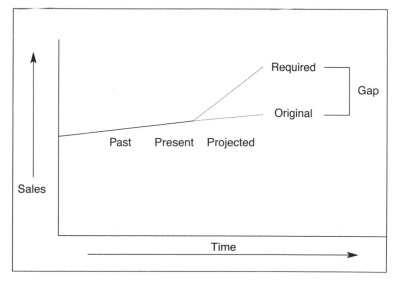

Figure 3.9   A revised sales forecast showing required and originally projected growth

Table 3.1   Sales projection for the UK

<table>
<tr><td colspan="7" align="center">THE EQUIPMENT MANUFACTURING COMPANY
SALES FIGURES (Historical and Forecast)</td></tr>
<tr><td>Sales Area:</td><td>UK</td><td></td><td></td><td></td><td></td><td></td></tr>
<tr><td></td><td colspan="3" align="center">◄——— Actual ———►</td><td colspan="3" align="center">◄——— Forecast ———►</td></tr>
<tr><td>Year
(all values in £k)</td><td>20X3</td><td>20X4</td><td>20X5</td><td>20X6</td><td>20X7</td><td>20X8</td></tr>
<tr><td>Filters</td><td>200</td><td>450</td><td>600</td><td>750</td><td>900</td><td>1,050</td></tr>
<tr><td>Valves</td><td>1,400</td><td>1,200</td><td>1,000</td><td>1,060</td><td>1,151</td><td>1,287</td></tr>
<tr><td>Components</td><td>300</td><td>350</td><td>400</td><td>450</td><td>525</td><td>600</td></tr>
<tr><td>Total</td><td>1,900</td><td>2,000</td><td>2,000</td><td>2,260</td><td>2,576</td><td>2,937</td></tr>
</table>

The next stage is to break this gap down into its constituent parts. Firstly we split it into inflationary growth (price increase) and volume growth.

gap   =   £937,000
price increase =   £253,000
volume increase =   £684,000

If we can double ball valve sales in the water industry this will add:

£300,000 – £150,000 = £150,000

If we can treble sales of packages this will add:

£500,000 – £140,000 = £360,000

We also intend to double filter sales to the water industry. This would add £400,000, but £360,000 of this is already included in 'packages'. Since component sales are basically spare filter cartridges, sales will certainly increase by more than £40,000 as a result of the number of packages sold. The objective 'to double filter sales to the water industry' can therefore be increased. The increase in component sales will be about £150,000.

Doubling sales in Scotland/NI will also add £50,000 to turnover.

This translates into:

price increase	=	£235,000
ball valves – water	=	£150,000
packages	=	£360,000
filter cartridges	=	£150,000
sales Scotland/NI	=	£50,000
total increase	=	£945,000

Our objectives would therefore close the gap, but only just. It is always wise to have something in reserve, since not all strategies and action plans will bring in the full return that we expect from them.

What is a marketing strategy?

Marketing strategies are the means by which marketing objectives will be achieved. It is important to understand what strategy is and how it differs from tactics. *Strategies* are the broad methods chosen to achieve specific objectives. They describe the means of achieving the objectives in the timescale required. They do not include the detail of the individual courses of action that will be followed on a day-to-day basis: these are *tactics*.

Marketing strategies relate to general policies for the following:

- **Products**
  - **changing product portfolio/mix;**
  - **dropping, adding or modifying products;**
  - **changing design, quality or performance;**
  - **consolidating/standardising.**

- Price
  - changing price, terms or conditions for particular product groups in particular market segments;
  - skimming policies;
  - penetration policies;
  - discount policies.
- Promotion
  - changing selling/salesforce organisation;
  - changing advertising or sales promotion;
  - changing public relations policy;
  - increasing/decreasing exhibition coverage.
- Distribution
  - changing channels;
  - improving service.

There are a number of different types of strategies:

- *Defensive strategies* – designed to prevent loss of existing customers;
- *Developing strategies* – designed to offer existing customers a wider range of your products or services;
- *Attacking strategies* – designed to generate business through new customers.

A useful way of looking at the types of strategy that may be available is to use a matrix that was developed by Ansoff, as shown in Figure 3.10.

It can be seen from this matrix that the least risky way to try to expand your business is in the areas you know best – ie with your existing products in your existing markets.

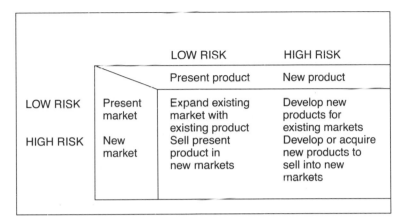

Figure 3.10   Ansoff Matrix – the risks of various strategies

Pricing strategies

There are many types of pricing strategies and tactics that can be considered. Most can, however, be broadly classified as either skimming policies or penetration policies.

- *Skimming* – This involves entering the market at a high price level and 'skimming' off as much profit as possible. As competition enters the market, the price level would be adjusted as necessary.
- *Penetration* – This is the opposite of skimming. With this type of strategy a company sets the price low deliberately. A penetration policy encourages more customers to purchase the product, which increases the company's sales turnover and also its market share.

We will now consider the strategies that The Equipment Manufacturing Company intends to adopt in order to achieve the objectives of its UK marketing plan.

In the scope of the UK plan they intend to concentrate mainly on expanding their existing markets with their existing products.

They will also expand the sales of the new product packages into existing markets. These are low risk strategies. They accept the need for new products and product improvements, but more work needs to be carried out to identify what is required. The main products to be considered are the ball valves and the 'type S' filters. They will carry out customer/competitor surveys over the next six months to define the market requirements for the new products. The products will then be developed. Since this will take at least 18 months, it is intended that the UK marketing plan will be revised in 12 months' time when the situation is clearer. The UK marketing plan will concentrate on areas of organisation and sales coverage that clearly need attention and the strategies being adopted are mainly *developing and attacking* strategies.

The key strategies for the Equipment Manufacturing Company for its UK plan are listed below:

- **Products**
  - **package products (ball valves with filters);**
  - **design new ball valve;**
  - **design replacement for 'type S' filters.**
- **Pricing**
  - **additional discount will be offered for online purchases to encourage use of our online shop;**
  - **penetration policy will be adopted with packages since these will help us to sell more valves;**
  - **penetration policy will be adopted on 'type K' filters since these generate a large proportion of replacement cartridges.**
- **Promotion**
  - **change salesforce organisation;**
  - **recruit additional sales personnel;**
  - **restructure sales management;**
  - **increase advertising;**
  - **increase exhibition coverage;**
  - **use mailshots/e-mailshots;**
  - **update and expand website;**
  - **add 'web analytics' for e-marketing.**

- Distribution
  - change distribution;
  - appoint distributor sales manager;
  - increase own sales coverage;
  - expand online shop.

Exercise

Now prepare some preliminary strategies for your marketing plan.

Our preliminary strategies are:

Products

_____

_____

_____

Price

_____

_____

_____

Promotion

_____

_____

_____

Distribution

_____

_____

_____

Action plans

Once you have selected the outline strategies and tactics to achieve your marketing objectives, you need to turn these strategies into programmes or action plans that will enable you to give clear instructions to your staff.

Each action plan should include:

- **current position – where you are now;**
- **aims – what to do/where do you want to go;**
- **action – what you need to do to get there;**
- **person responsible – who will do it;**
- **start date;**
- **finish date;**
- **budgeted cost.**

Each action plan would need to be broken down into its component parts. Table 3.2 shows a suggested layout for an action plan for The Equipment Manufacturing Company. This plan is to carry out the strategy of 'carry out an e-mailshot'. The e-mailshot is for filter packages aimed at the water-treatment industry.

Table 3.2   Presentation of an action plan

ACTION PLAN – e-mail shot – filters packages						
DEPARTMENT: SALES						
Aim	Current position	Action	By	Start	Finish	Cost
Carry out e-mail shot	Need 'opt in' e-mail list of target companies	Purchase list	ALT	9.1.X6	16.1.X6	£200
	Need material for website	Prepare material for website	JDT	9.1.X6	20.2.X6	£300
	Need link to website	Create link on e-mail	JDT	21.2.X6	21.2.X6	£10
		Send out	ILH	27.2.X6	27.2.X6	£100

Each of the actions on this action plan could be broken down into a number of parts. In the preparation of the material for the website there would be a number of stages, including:

- **liaising with the production department on when a completed filter package will be available;**
- **having the filter package photographed;**
- **liaising with the engineering department to prepare technical information to include in the web page text;**

- writing the text;
- preparing preliminary layout of text and images on the test web page;
- proofreading the test web page and checking the web links;
- publishing the web page live.

After scheduling your activities on the basis of action plans you should combine the individual action plans and programmes into larger functional programmes (product, pricing, promotion, distribution). These functional programmes would appear in the marketing plan. They would then be developed into an overall schedule – a master programme that can be used for controlling the implementation of the plan. This is the schedule of what/where/how in the written plan. Although it would only be the larger functional programmes and the master programme schedule that would appear in the written plan, each of the smaller plans and programmes would need to be communicated to those who have to carry them out.

Summary

Setting marketing objectives is the key step in the preparation of a marketing plan. Marketing objectives are what we want to achieve with our plan. They must be definable and quantifiable and should be expressed in terms of values or market shares. Before setting your marketing objectives it is important to understand your present position with regard to products and markets. You should look at your product portfolio with regard to product life cycles and cash generation. Although all forecasts are based on an analysis of past sales, they should also take into account the total potential market, the existing market share and the life cycle of the product.

Marketing *objectives* should be difficult but achievable. The aim is to set objectives that are a challenge, but that can be achieved with effort. They must be motivating rather than discouraging.

Marketing *strategies* are the methods by which you achieve your marketing objectives. They relate to *products*, *pricing*, *advertising/promotion* and *distribution*.

As there will always be a huge range of potential strategies available to any company, those that will best satisfy your objectives and which can be effectively implemented using the resources and capabilities of your company should be selected.

Strategies must be converted into programmes or action plans in order that they may be carried out. These individual action plans are then combined into larger functional programmes which in turn are combined in the master programme schedule. It is the larger functional programmes and the master programme schedule which appear in the written marketing plan.

Distribution, promotion and budgets

Promotion means getting the right message to the right people. It involves personal selling, advertising and sales promotion. But before you can plan your advertising and sales promotion you need to select the right channels for your product and your business from those available. This is part of the distribution plan, which will always be part of any marketing plan.

The distribution plan

The physical distribution of goods is only one aspect of distribution as defined by marketing planners. Distribution involves:

- **marketing channels;**
- **physical distribution;**
- **customer service.**

Marketing channels

Marketing channels are the means that a company can select to get into contact with its potential customers. If its potential customers are unaware of the product, they will not buy it. There are a wide variety of different channels that a company can use. Figure 4.1 shows a typical selection of available marketing channels.

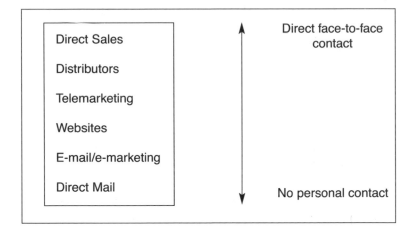

Figure 4.1   Marketing channels

Direct sales is an expensive channel to operate and is mainly restricted to high value industrial goods. The bulk of advertising expenditure is used on consumer goods, particularly low value, repeat buy items such as food and household consumables. Consumer goods are usually sold through distributors, wholesalers and retailers rather than through direct selling, but it is usually still necessary for the company to have a salesforce to sell to these distributors, wholesalers and retailers.

The characteristics of the product you are selling will have a considerable influence on the mix of marketing channels that you finally select (see Figure 4.2). The number of levels of

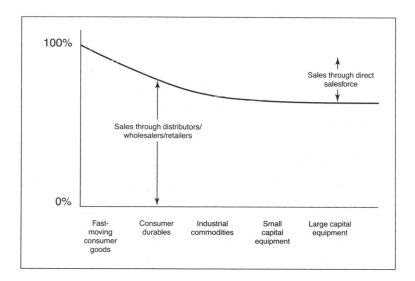

Figure 4.2   The Influence of product characteristics on distribution channels

channels of distribution will also affect prices because of the level of discounts that will need to be built into the price structure.

Direct sales

In a perfect world direct selling with the salesperson face to face with the customer would give a company the maximum possibility of getting the message across and closing the sale. In the real world this is just not cost effective and all companies employ a mixture of direct and indirect sales techniques.

The advantages of personal selling are:

- it allows two-way communication between the buyer and seller;
- the salesperson can tailor the presentation to the individual needs of the customer;

- the salesperson comes to know and be known by the customers;
- the salesperson can negotiate directly on price, delivery, discounts;
- the salesperson can close the sale;
- the salesperson can monitor customer satisfaction levels.

Distributors

In consumer goods industries distributors could be retailers, wholesalers or even companies who sell to wholesalers. For industrial goods, it is not usual to use wholesale/retail outlets in the same way. Direct sales to customers generally make up a larger proportion of sales than with consumer goods, but the use of commission agents and distributors is widespread. A distributor takes over the selling role of the manufacturer and most distributors have their own salesforce dealing with customers.

Distributors would normally be expected to hold enough stock to service the geographical area for which they are responsible. Most distributors sell a range of products, so a product will not get the exclusive treatment through a distributor's salesforce that it would through a company's own salesforce.

A direct salesforce can be structured:

- by product;
- by area;
- by account.

Distributors can also be appointed on the same basis.

Telemarketing

Telemarketing involves selling and marketing by telephone rather than by direct physical contact. Generally, it has been found that telemarketing is most effective when it supplements the field salesforce activity rather than completely replacing it. It is cost effective because 40–50 telephone calls can be made per day whereas 6–10 personal visits per day is normal for direct sales calls. The main advantages of telemarketing are:

- **lower cost than direct salesforce;**
- **it frees up the salesperson's time by reducing routine calling activity;**
- **it increases frequency of customer contact;**
- **it allows dormant accounts to be revived;**
- **in some cases it can be farmed out to a professional telemarketing company.**

Currently telemarketing uses telephone landlines. This is set to change within the next decade. Before the year 2000, virtually all telephone users had a landline, even though the use of mobile phones was increasing. By 2009 about 12 per cent of households in the United Kingdom and more than 20 per cent of households in the United States had no landline and only a mobile phone. Some analysts estimate that by 2015 the majority of households will have only mobile phones and that the last landline will be switched off in about 2025.

Websites

The internet provides a major new sales channel for all types of products. Most companies of any size have online purchasing. Major supermarket chains now encourage online purchasing and customers can order their weekly shopping online and have it delivered to their door. Hotel rooms and packaged holidays can also be booked online, either directly with the hotel/package tour provider, or at specialist sites, such as www.expedia.co.uk. Books and CDs can be purchased from a number of sites including www.amazon.co.uk. Computers, cars and electrical goods can now all be ordered online.

One effect of these websites is to drive down prices, because the consumer can now surf the web and compare prices from different suppliers. But there is an additional advantage to companies in terms of getting the best out of their websites and in using them for sales promotion. The use of web analytics software means that companies can now track which pages of their websites are most popular and which promotions are clicked on most – basically, which parts seem to attract users and which parts don't. They can track where users enter and where they leave, where they come from (which search engines, etc) and where they go next, how long they stay on the site and how many pages they look at while they are there. This is far more detailed feedback than is available in other media.

E-mail/e-marketing

E-marketing and web analytics have brought about big changes in marketing tactics. E-mail is the perfect vehicle to build lifetime relationships with customers. There are a large number of e-marketing companies that can supply permission-based technology to help businesses communicate, and build or add to their existing database of potential and existing customers, creating targeted direct e-marketing campaigns with information and offerings specific to each customer's interests. Permission marketing can turn online visitors into lifetime customers by allowing regular communication with both existing and prospective customers. Giving consumers total control of the messages they receive is the future of direct marketing on the internet. Permission marketing is the ideal solution to personalise relationships and secure continued customer support.

With opt-in e-mail, responses (5 to 15 per cent) are far greater than those from banner advertising (0.5 per cent), or traditional direct mail (1 to 3 per cent). In addition to a greater response rate, a direct e-mail marketing campaign costs only a fraction of the cost of more traditional methods of marketing.

E-mail bulletins can even track how many users open the e-mails and what, if anything, they click on in the bulletin. This is far more effective at collating customer information than direct mail.

Direct mail

Direct mail includes mail-order business and the use of mailshots. Mailshots involve sending information on a specific product by mail to potential customers on a mailing list. They rely on the accuracy of the mailing list used, and a low return rate (1 to 3 per cent) is considered quite normal. They are still very popular because small items or samples can be sent with the mailshot – something that is not possible with e-mail. But in many cases they are being superseded by e-mailshots on the grounds of cost and efficiency.

Physical distribution, warehousing and factory location

Physical distribution involves not only the holding of stock, but also communicating within the distribution network and the way that the product is packaged for distribution. The proximity of the factory to its markets is more important with high-bulk–low-value goods than with sophisticated capital goods, but stocking at the factory, at warehouses or logistics centres is an important part of distribution strategy that will determine whether you can give as good a service as your competitors – or better.

Customer service

For the distribution plan we are only interested in the aspects of customer service that affect distribution. This really relates to the level of availability of the product to the customer. Distribution is about getting the product to the right place (for the customer) at the right time. Theoretically you want to offer your customers 100 per cent availability of the product. In practice this is not possible. It is necessary to find a balance between the costs and benefits involved. The costs of extra availability cannot exceed the extra revenue that will be gained as a result.

Exercise

Below we consider the *marketing channels* and *physical distribution* used by The Equipment Manufacturing Company in the UK.

Marketing channels

The Equipment Manufacturing Company uses a mixture of direct sales (to large key accounts and contracting companies) and distributors (who hold stock of valves/filters and spares). It has recently started to use telemarketing to follow up dormant accounts. It has also set up an online shop on its website.

Physical distribution

The company manufactures valves at its factory in Manchester and filters at its factory in the South of England and holds a stock of components and spare parts at the factory. It does not stock finished valves or filters and only supplies to order. The company's distributors operate on a discount level of 30 per cent from the company's list price and this finances the stocks of equipment that they hold in stock. The company uses local haulage contractors for deliveries of finished goods. More urgent deliveries are made using nationwide overnight services such as DHL, UPS and TNT. The company operates an MRP (Materials Resource Planning) system with a computer database that includes order processing and invoicing. In addition the company operates a computer database for its distribution network and can advise one distributor where he can find a component (with another distributor) if he does not have it in stock. With the agreement of their distributors, the company is making this database accessible to all distributors via its website (this part of the website will be restricted and will only be accessible to authorised company and distributor personnel who will have to log in individually).

Now consider the marketing channels and distribution used by your own company for the products and areas covered by your marketing plan. Detail these below:

Marketing channels

_____

_____

_____

Physical distribution/logistics

_____

_____

_____

In the distribution plan it is necessary to consider if a change in marketing channels or physical distribution is necessary. For The Equipment Manufacturing Company sales of valves are concentrated in the Midlands and the North of England – where the company's distribution is strong. Its sales in Wales, Scotland and Northern Ireland are minimal. The distributors in these areas should be evaluated and possibly replaced. It may also be worthwhile considering acquiring one or more distributors to give the company its own logistics base in a particular area.

The advertising and promotions plan

The advertising and promotions plan involves personnel, advertising and promotions.

Personnel

Once you have selected your mix of distribution channels you can decide on the personnel requirements of the plan. As shown in Figure 4.2 on page 61, your product will determine to some extent the channels that you use. The channels will determine to some extent the type of sales organisation that you need. In the situation analysis we carried out a SWOT analysis for the sales organisation of The Equipment Manufacturing Company (Figure 2.5). This indicated the weaknesses that need to be addressed and the opportunities that we can take. We now need to detail the existing sales structure and the proposed structure for the plan. In doing this we need to indicate which personnel are existing and which are additional (or replacements!).

The existing UK sales organisation of The Equipment Manufacturing Company is shown in Figure 4.3.

Figure 4.3   Existing sales organisation

With this structure, the sales engineers are selling to large key accounts and contracting companies and the UK sales manager is running the salesforce and distribution. The industry specialists are sales engineers who have both area and industry responsibilities. This structure lacks focus. There are a number of different ways that it could be restructured to improve focus. My proposal is shown in Figure 4.4.

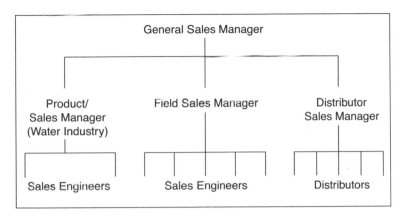

Figure 4.4   Proposed new sales organisation

In this structure, the general sales manager and distributor sales manager are new personnel who need to be recruited. The UK sales manager has become the field sales manager. Field sales is the job he does best. The sales engineer who is the expert in the water industry becomes the product/sales manager for the water industry and a separate salesforce is being created to develop water industry sales. The list of new and existing sales personnel is shown in Figure 4.5.

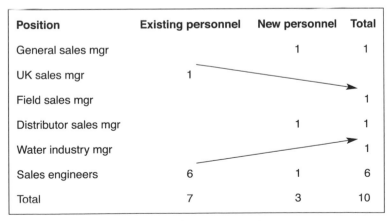

Position	Existing personnel	New personnel	Total
General sales mgr		1	1
UK sales mgr	1		
Field sales mgr			1
Distributor sales mgr		1	1
Water industry mgr			1
Sales engineers	6	1	6
Total	7	3	10

Figure 4.5   New and existing sales personnel

Exercise

Now consider the sales organisation for your plan. Draw up the existing organisation structure, detail its strengths and weaknesses, analyse the focus that you have and the focus that you need. Draw up your new structure and if it is different from the existing structure note the new personnel required.

_____

_____

_____

Advertising and promotions

The purpose of advertising is to get a message across to the customer. Advertising operates at three levels – it _informs_, it _persuades_ and it _reinforces_. Advertising to inform normally relates to the promotion of new products and services. Advertising to persuade is what most people understand as advertising. There is also the public relations side of advertising – promotional public relations. This includes media relations and exhibitions.

Because advertising on television and in the national press is very expensive, most television and national press advertising relates to consumer goods with large annual sales or services such as banking and insurance. The advertising of industrial and capital goods uses much narrower and more specific outlets such as industry-specific magazines or websites. Repeat advertising is more effective than one-off advertisements. The same advert repeated every week or every month in a limited number of outlets is more effective than different one-off adverts in a wide range of outlets.

Similarly, industrial products are normally exhibited at exhibitions that are specific for that industry rather than general trade fairs. Most industrial companies now also use their website to provide information on their products and to publicise new products and sales successes. The advantage of a website is that even small companies can give the impression of being large and knowledgeable.

In addition to company websites, there is now also a range of independent websites for specific types of industrial equipment (pumps and valves, vacuum equipment, mixing equipment) or industries, (pulp and paper, chemical manufacturing, water and waste treatment).

The Equipment Manufacturing Company is targeting the water industry. Table 4.1 and Figure 4.6 show a press advertising schedule and exhibition cost schedule it has prepared.

Table 4.1   Advertising schedule

ADVERTISING															
Application: Water Industry			Year: 20X6												
MEDIA	No	Rate per insertion £	Total cost £	J	F	M	A	M	J	J	A	S	O	N	D
Water and Waste Treatment	2	1,800	3,600				X				X				
Water Services	2	1,500	3,000					X				X			
Water Bulletin	3	800	2,400			X			X			X			
Water products. com	1	2,000	2,000	X	X	X	X	X	X	X	X	X	X	X	X
TOTAL COST			11,000												

The advertising schedule includes the annual cost of subscribing to the website www.waterproducts.com. This is a website that specialises in products used in the water and waste treatment industries. Descriptions of their individual products for the water industry are shown on the site and pdf files of their technical literature and datasheets can be downloaded from it. The site has a 'web analytics' system and can provide the company with lists of users who visit the site and details of which of the company's products they have looked at. The company will also be carrying out some targeted mail/e-mailshots and expanding its website to include 'web analytics' for e-marketing. The costs of these items will go into the advertising and promotions plan.

EXHIBITION COSTS
Name of exhibition: IWEX Location: NEC Birmingham Date: 6th–8th November 20X6 Stand size: 64 m² (8 m × 8 m) Stand Contractor: Exhibition Contractors Ltd
Costs £ Stand space rental   8,000 Design, supply and build   10,000 Artwork, photographic panels   5,000 Rental of carpets, furniture, lights, phone, etc   3,000 Hotel bills/expenditure for stand staff   2,000 Total   28,000

Figure 4.6   Schedule of expenditure for a major exhibition

Exercise

Prepare similar schedules and costs for promotions that you intend to include in your plan.

_____

_____

_____

_____

Costs and budgets

In carrying out the marketing planning process and preparing your plan, you have already seen how to decide on strategies and to prepare the action plans to enable you to carry out your strategies and achieve your objectives. You have seen how realistic objectives can be set. But what about your strategies and action plans? They may be feasible, but are they cost-effective? If the cost of implementing your strategies and carrying out your action plans is greater than the contribution to company profits resulting from the additional sales forecast in the plan, you might as well forget the plan now – unless you can devise other strategies to achieve the same objectives.

How can you decide if your marketing plan is viable? Only by preparing a partial profit and loss account. For sales personnel, this can be the most difficult part of the whole process. All companies have a particular way that they put together the financial data that goes into their profit and loss account. It is wise to involve someone from your finance and accounting department to help you to prepare the partial profit and loss account that you need for your plan.

Profit and loss account

The profit and loss account is a summary of the success or failure of the transactions of a company over a period of time. It lists income generated and costs incurred. From the point of view of our marketing plan, we are not interested in anything below the line of operating profit, because our marketing activities will only affect items reported above this line in the profit and loss account. The profit and loss account for The Equipment Manufacturing Company down to the operating profit level is shown in Figure 4.7.

It is important to understand the key items reported in the profit and loss account.

			£000
	Turnover		6,000
less	Cost of sales		4,000
	Gross profit		2,000
less	Distribution costs	100	
	Operating expenses	850	
			950
	Operating profit		1,050

Figure 4.7   Profit and loss account for The Equipment Manufacturing Company

Turnover

The turnover represents the total amount of revenue earned during the year from the company's normal trading operations.

Cost of sales

This represents the direct costs of making the product that is sold. The costs are primarily labour and materials.

Gross profit

When the cost of sales is removed from the turnover, the resultant figure is the gross profit. This gives a direct comparison between what the product can be sold for and what it costs to make. This 'margin' has to be sufficient to cover all of the costs and overheads incurred in running the business.

Other costs

These would include distribution costs, administration and operating expenses. This includes the cost of running the sales and marketing department together with advertising and promotional costs. It would also include head office salaries, rates, electricity, depreciation and the cost of research and development.

Operating profit

This is the key figure in the accounts as far as we are concerned. It is the net result of trading for the year, when total sales revenue is compared with the expenses incurred in earning that revenue. It is the ultimate measure of whether it has been worth while staying in business.

Exercise

Before you start budgeting for your marketing plan you need to familiarise yourself with the accounting practices used within your own company or business unit. If you do not already have them, you should obtain copies of your company's profit and loss account and get your accounts department to explain how the distribution costs and operating expenses are calculated and allocated.

Budgeting the cost of a marketing plan

Your marketing plan is part of your company business plan. Individual marketing plans are ultimately collated into the overall company marketing plan. The principles are the same whether you are preparing the sales budget for the overall company marketing plan or calculating the effect of an individual marketing plan. However, in budgeting and evaluating individual marketing plans, we only need to consider part of the company budgeting process. This is shown in Figure 4.8.

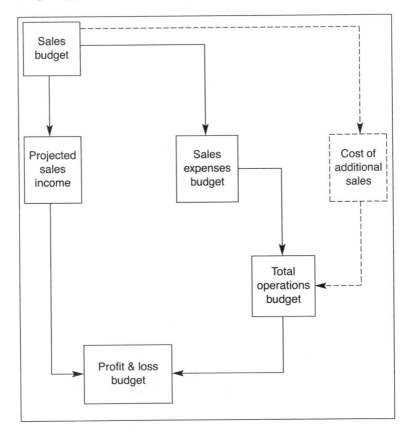

Figure 4.8 Budgeting for additional sales

It is only if your product is a new one or if you are forecasting considerable increases in business from your plan that major capital investment may also be required. Obviously, if your plan includes an increase in field sales personnel, there will be additional requirements for company cars and laptop computers which must be budgeted for.

With a marketing plan for an individual product or market, we are not considering the total company turnover and costs, but only the additional turnover generated by the plan and the costs associated with its implementation.

There are a number of techniques that allow you to predict whether the extra business that you will generate from your plan will be profitable or not. One of the simplest is to cost up all of the expenses that you intend to incur in implementing your plan and to compare these with the contribution that will be generated by the additional sales turnover that will result from your plan. For individual plans this method is quite adequate and we will use it here. (When a new product is being introduced more complex techniques such as break-even analysis or payback analysis can also be used. These techniques are explained further in *The Marketing Plan*, also published by Kogan Page.)

It is necessary to cost up all of the action plans for all of the different strategies through which you intend to achieve your objectives.

First let us look at the operating expenses budget for the UK sales department of The Equipment Manufacturing Company before the implementation of the marketing plan. This is shown in Table 4.2.

Now we will prepare a partial profit and loss account for The Equipment Manufacturing Company based on the *additional costs* of implementing the UK marketing plan.

In preparing this profit and loss account budget, we start at the top with the forecast sales. Here we are only showing the *additional sales*. The cost of sales is the direct cost, in materials and labour, of making the budgeted amount of product sold. The gross profit is the 'margin' to cover other costs and to contribute to profits.

In carrying out the marketing plan, the operating expenses incurred will relate to different departments. Most of the costs will relate to the sales and marketing department, but they will include administrative recharges for the management of company cars, allocation of office space (rent/rates/heating/lighting), and computer management and maintenance.

The costs incurred by the sales and marketing department represent the cost of extra items such as literature, advertising and exhibitions and the cost of salaries and travelling expenses related to the additional staff included in the plan. They will include the costs of the advertising campaign and exhibition for the water industry shown in Table 4.1 (page 71) and Figure 4.6 (page 72). The costs of the existing salesforce (shown in Table 4.2) are already included in the overall company profit and loss budget and do not therefore need to be included again in this partial profit and loss budget.

Table 4.2   Example of operating expenses budget

OPERATING EXPENSES BUDGET FOR 20X6 Department: UK Sales					
Item	20X5 expenses	Inflation	Growth	Other	20X6
	£k	%	£k	£k	£k	£k
Salaries	160	3	4.8	75.0		239.8
Recruitment	3	3	0.1	6.0		9.1
Travel/entertaining	30	3	0.9	7.0		37.9
Car costs	14	3	0.4	6.0		20.4
Advertising	10	3	0.3	11.0		21.3
Exhibitions	10	3	0.3		28.0	38.3
Literature	10	3	0.3		5.0	15.3
Sundry items	10	3	0.3			10.3
Total	247	3	7.4	105.0	33.0	392.4

The partial profit and loss account for the additional sales included in the UK marketing plan is shown in Table 4.3.

It can be seen that the plan shows a loss in its first year and only breaks even in year two. This is quite normal. It would be nice if we could always plan to break even straight away, but in the real world it is often necessary to invest first and reap the rewards later. It would be of concern if break even was later than the second year because it would then become a vanishing horizon. In this case it would be wise to reconsider the plan.

Table 4.3 Effect on profit and loss account of additional operating expenses for implementing UK marketing plan

	20X6 £k	20X7 £k	20X8 £k
Invoiced sales	260.0	576.0	937.0
Cost of sales	158.6	339.8	534.1
Gross profit	101.4	236.2	402.9
Sales & Marketing costs			
Salaries	75.0	78.0	81.1
Recruitment	6.0		
Travel/entertaining	7.0	7.6	7.9
Car costs	6.0	6.2	6.5
Advertising	11.0	11.5	12.0
Exhibitions	28.0		15.0
Literature	5.0	25.0	20.0
Sundry items		5.0	6.0
Total sales costs	138.0	133.3	148.5
Administration costs	20.0	20.8	21.6
Data processing costs	5.0	5.5	6.0
Distribution costs	6.9	7.2	7.5
Total operating expenses (relating to plan)	169.9	166.8	183.6
Operating profit (relating to plan)	(68.5)	69.4	219.3

Exercise

Now detail the initial operating expenses budget for the sales department in your plan. Also prepare a partial profit and loss account for the additional sales and additional costs included in your plan.

Summary

Implementing a marketing plan requires communication, which means getting the right message over to the right people. This involves personal selling, advertising and sales promotion.

Before you can put together your advertising and promotions plan, you need to select the right marketing channels for your product and business from those available. This is part of the distribution plan which also includes the physical distribution of goods and customer service. The advertising and promotions plan should include details of the present structure of your sales organisation and any changes proposed for the implementation of the marketing plan. It should include the details, schedules and costs of the advertising and sales promotion campaigns that are included in the marketing plan.

Because there is no point in proceeding with your marketing plan unless it is going to increase company profits, you need to be able to evaluate its cost-effectiveness. You need to consider the additional turnover and contribution generated by your plan and the costs associated with its implementation. This involves the preparation of a partial profit and loss budget.

Writing the plan

Now that you have collected all of the information for your plan, you can prepare the written document and set about communicating it effectively to the relevant people in your company.

The written plan should only contain the key information that needs to be communicated – it should be clear and concise, and excessive or irrelevant detail should be excluded. The bulk of the internal and external market research information collected in the course of the preparation of the plan should not be included in the written plan since this would only confuse the reader. The detail of all of the individual action plans would also be excluded from the main document – although a summary of very important action plans may be included. Other key information that you want to include should be put in appendices and not in the main document.

The written plan must be clear, concise and easy to read. The following points give some guidelines:

- **Start each complete section on a new page – even if this means that some pages have only five or ten lines of text on them.**

- When listing key points, use double spacing.
- Do not try to cram too many figures onto one page.
- Do not reduce the size of documents used in the plan to a point where they become difficult to read.
- Use a reasonable font size when printing the document.
- If the plan is too long it will just not be read, so be ruthless and cut out unnecessary text.
- Do not use jargon that may not be understood by all those who will receive the plan, and be sure to expand any abbreviations to their full form at their first appearance.

If you are careful in the way that you write the plan you can use many of the individual sections as presentation slides.

You should start with a table of contents which will enable the reader to quickly locate the various sections of the plan. Figure 5.1 shows how the table of contents should be set out.

CONTENTS		
Section		Page
1	INTRODUCTION	2
2	EXECUTIVE SUMMARY	3
3	SITUATION ANALYSIS – Assumptions	4
	– Sales (History/Budget)	5
	– Strategic Markets	7
	– Key Products	9
	– Key Sales Areas	11
4	MARKETING OBJECTIVES	13
5	MARKETING STRATEGIES	14
6	SCHEDULES	18
7	SALES PROMOTION	19
8	BUDGETS	20
9	PROFIT AND LOSS ACCOUNT	22
10	CONTROLS	23
11	UPDATE PROCEDURES	24
	APPENDIX 1	26
	APPENDIX 2	32

Figure 5.1   Contents list of a complete marketing plan

Depending on the scope of your plan, you may need to omit or combine certain sections.

Introduction

This gives the background to the plan, and the reasons for its preparation, and outlines its purposes and uses.

The introduction to the UK plan for The Equipment Manufacturing Company is as follows:

> UK sales have stagnated in recent years. The company has always sold a reasonable amount of product into the water industry, but it has never been a key activity area. Because of this, we knew little of the industry or of the potential in it for our product. With the enforcement of EU directives for water treatment and sewage disposal, the industry is now again carrying out a major capital improvement programme. It was therefore felt by the sales and marketing director that we needed to analyse our position in the market and prepare for growth to take advantage of the increased level of spending by the industry.

Exercise

Prepare an introduction for your plan:

_____

_____

_____

Executive summary

The summary should present the key points of the plan in a clear
and concise form. It should not be too long or verbose. All
personnel reading this plan should be able to understand the
essence of the plan from this summary.

The summary should always include:

- **the underlying assumptions on which the plan is based;**
- **the objectives of the plan;**
- **the timescale over which the plan will be implemented.**

Although you can draft out an executive summary at any time,
you cannot finalise the text until the plan is complete.

The executive summary of the UK marketing plan for The
Equipment Manufacturing Company is given below:

> Although our total sales in the UK market have fallen, sales of
> filters have tripled in the last three years. The increase in
> filter sales has been mainly into the water industry. Our
> problem area has been ball valves where we only have a 10
> per cent market share, with low sales in the water industry.
> We currently have market shares in the water industry of 10
> per cent for filters and 5 per cent for valves. We believe that if
> economic conditions remain stable, we will be able to gain
> market share in this expanding market. Also, the packaging
> of our filters and valves together will give us a competitive
> advantage.
>
> The objective of this plan is to achieve 10 per cent growth
> in UK sales in real terms over the next three years, doubling
> our water industry market share for filters to 20 per cent
> and doubling our market share for ball valves to 10 per
> cent of the projected market in 20X8. In doing so, we in-
> tend to increase UK overall gross margins from 39 per cent to
> 43 per cent by 20X8. This plan details how this can be
> achieved with an investment in personnel and resources, but

without any major additional investment in plant and machinery.

Exercise

Sketch out below your first attempt at an executive summary for your plan. This should then be checked and, if necessary, amended when your plan is complete:

_____

_____

_____

Situation analysis

In the written plan, the situation analysis should include only the summaries of the external and internal marketing research and the key resulting SWOT analysis. These are included under the headings:

- **assumptions;**
- **a summary of historical and budgeted sales;**
- **a review of strategic markets;**
- **a review of key products;**
- **a review of key sales areas.**

There will be some overlap between the reviews of strategic markets, key products and key sales areas, because it is possible to show the mix in different ways. The important thing is to present the information in a manner that highlights the key points you are trying to convey to those who read the plan. Often the SWOT analyses are put together in the appendix.

Assumptions

These are the key facts and assumptions on which the plan is based. They should be few in number and should relate only to the key issues which would significantly affect the likelihood of the plan's marketing objectives being achieved.

Each assumption should be a brief factual statement. For example:

- The £/$ exchange rate will remain in the range $1.50 to $1.70:£1 for the next 12 months.
- Interest rates will not increase by more than 1 per cent over the next three years.
- Company wage increases will not exceed inflation over the next three years.

The Equipment Manufacturing Company has made the following assumptions with regard to its UK marketing plan:

- Inflation will remain at 3 per cent in 20X6, rising to 4 per cent in 20X7 and 20X8.
- Company wage increases will not exceed inflation over the next three years.
- The pound sterling will not strengthen against either the euro or the US$ during the timescale of the plan.
- There will be no delay in the timescale for the UK water industry to implement the EU directives on drinking-water and effluent.

Exercise

List the assumptions that you will include in your
marketing plan:

- _____
- _____
- _____
- _____

Sales

In this section you should include historical sales going back
three years together with sales forecasts for the next three years.
Unless you state otherwise, it will be assumed that the years
shown in your forecast are calendar years. You should use
invoiced sales rather than order intake figures as the basis of the
plan, because other departments in the company, such as
production and finance, can only operate on sales figures. You
will, however, need to include order intake figures in your plan as
well, because these will be the order budgets that the sales
department will work to. More detail would normally be included
with regard to the next 12 months' sales forecast since this will
become the annual budget for the product or area covered by the
plan.

In this section under _Sales_ you would normally only include
the sales projection for the total area and products. A more
detailed breakdown into individual products and sub-areas
would be included under key products, key sales areas or in the
appendix to the plan. The format for setting out this information
follows the guidelines given in Chapter 2.

The sales projection for The Equipment Manufacturing
Company for the UK plan is shown in Table 5.1.

Exercise

Prepare a sales projection for your own company for your plan:

- _____
- _____
- _____

Table 5.1   Sales projection for the UK

THE EQUIPMENT MANUFACTURING COMPANY SALES FIGURES (Historical and Forecast)						

Sales Area:	UK					
		← Actual →			← Forecast →	
Year (all values in £k)	20X3	20X4	20X5	20X6	20X7	20X8
Filters	200	450	600	750	900	1,050
Valves	1,400	1,200	1,000	1,060	1,151	1,287
Components	300	350	400	450	525	600
Total	1,900	2,000	2,000	2,260	2,576	2,937

Strategic markets

In this section you should include historical information and forecasts for the company's sales in key industry sectors. The information can be presented in two ways:

1. showing the percentage of company sales into each market;
2. showing the percentage share of individual markets that the company believes that it has.

Only include your key markets – ideally this should be between three and six industries, because if you only sell to one industry you will be very vulnerable to changes or fluctuations within that industry.

This type of information can either be presented in tabular or graphical form. Tables 5.2 and 5.3 are representations for The Equipment Manufacturing Company in tabular form and Figure 5.2 in graphical form. You should also include some background notes on the key industries.

Table 5.2   Presentation of sales by strategic market

UK SALES – STRATEGIC MARKETS				
Product: Ball valves	**Actual – 20X5**		**Forecast – 20X8**	
Industry	£k	%	£k	%
Chem/Petrochem	360	36	430	33
Water	150	15	300	23
Paper	120	12	150	12
Food	80	8	90	7
Other	290	29	317	25
Total	1,000	100	1,287	100

Table 5.3   Presentation of sales and market share by strategic market

UK SALES – STRATEGIC MARKETS				
Product: Filters & components	**Actual – 20X5**		**Forecast – 20X8**	
Industry	£k	%	£k	%
Chem/Petrochem	200	20	250	15
Water	400	40	900	55
Paper	150	15	220	13
Other	250	25	280	17
Total	1,000	100	1,650	100

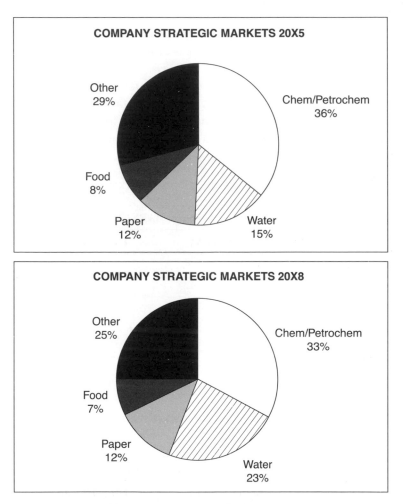

Figure 5.2   Graphical representation of The Equipment
Manufacturing Company's strategic markets for ball valves

The narrative included by The Equipment Manufacturing
Company in their UK plan is as follows:

Chemical/Petrochemical industry

The chemical/petrochemical industry is our biggest market worldwide. In the UK it accounts for more than 25 per cent of our total sales. Although it is a major source of revenue, the market has been hit hard by the move in refining capacity and heavy chemicals production out of high cost areas like Europe to the Far East. We will do well to hold our own in this industry in the UK over the next few years.

Similar notes are included for other key industries.

Exercise

Prepare information on your strategic markets for inclusion in your marketing plan:

_____

_____

_____

Key products

This section lists your key products and details technological and commercial factors relating to them. This would include the results of the SWOT analysis on your products and your competitors' products. The information could be presented in a similar format to the data on strategic markets, or it could be included in a product portfolio matrix. A SWOT analysis for a product and the product portfolio matrix for The Equipment Manufacturing Company are shown in Figures 5.3 and 5.4.

STRENGTHS	WEAKNESSES
■ Good range of sizes ■ Quality product ■ Solidly built	■ Limited range of materials ■ Heavier than competitors' products ■ High cost/high price
OPPORTUNITIES	THREATS
■ Source product from China ■ Develop new product	■ Cheap imports from Asia ■ Competing products in plastic materials

Figure 5.3 SWOT analysis for product – ball valves

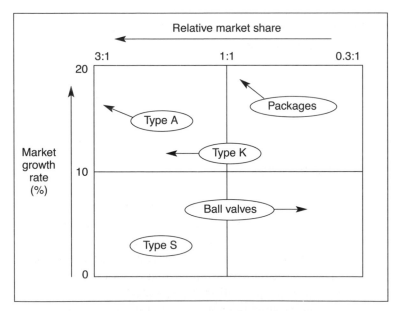

Figure 5.4 Portfolio matrix of The Equipment Manufacturing Company

The following narrative is included by The Equipment Manufacturing Company in their UK marketing plan:

> *Ball Valves*
> Our ball valve product is nearing the end of its useful life. We intend to carry out a customer/competitor survey over the next six months to define the market requirements for a new product. The development of the new product will take at least 18 months. In the meantime, we will continue to develop sales of the product as a component in our filter packages for the water industry.

Notes are also included on the company's ranges of filters.

Exercise

Prepare key product information for the products included in your plan:

_____

_____

_____

Key sales areas

This information is presented in the same way as the information on strategic markets, but gives the information relating to geographical areas instead of industry sectors. The information can be presented in tabular form as in Table 5.4 or in graphical form as in Figure 5.5.

Exercise

Prepare information on your own key sales areas:

_____

_____

_____

Table 5.4   Representation of key sales areas

THE EQUIPMENT MANUFACTURING COMPANY SALES FIGURES (Historical and Forecast)						

Sales Area: UK
Product: Ball valves

	◄── Actual ──►			◄── Forecast ──►		
Year (all values in £k)	20X3	20X4	20X5	20X6	20X7	20X8
South	295	250	230	240	250	260
Midlands	485	415	360	370	390	420
North	525	420	300	325	351	422
Wales	45	55	60	65	70	75
Scotland/NI	50	60	50	70	90	110
Total	1,400	1,200	1,000	1,070	1,151	1,287

In the narrative of your plan you should include relevant information on the size of each key market, growth rates, and your position in each market now and projected for the future. You should also include comments which may relate to your distributor, agent or other methods of distribution in that market.

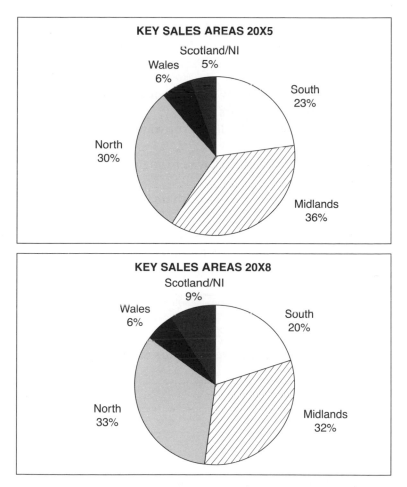

Figure 5.5 Graphical representation of key sales areas for ball valve sales for The Equipment Manufacturing Company

Marketing objectives

This is a list of the objectives that are to be achieved, quantified in terms of order intake, sales turnover, market share and profit.

In the written plan you should list your key objectives only. The key objectives are overall objectives.

The objectives included in the marketing plan for the UK for The Equipment Manufacturing Company are as follows:

- **To increase UK sales by 10 per cent per year in real terms for the next three years.**
- **To double ball valve sales to the water industry within three years.**
- **To increase sales of packages to 50 units within three years.**
- **To double market share for filters in the water industry by 20X8.**
- **To double distributor sales in Scotland and NI by 20X8.**
- **To increase overall gross margins from 39 per cent to 43 per cent by 20X8.**

Exercise

Now list the key objectives for your marketing plan:

_____

_____

_____

Marketing strategies

You should indicate whether you are adopting defensive, developing or attacking strategies – or a mixture of different types. The individual strategies should then be listed under the headings of the four main elements of the marketing mix:

- **Strategies relating to products.**
- **Strategies relating to pricing.**

- Strategies relating to advertising/promotion.
- Strategies relating to distribution.

There may be some overlap between the individual categories, but this does not matter so long as all of the strategies are listed.

In their plan, The Equipment Manufacturing Company are adopting a mixture of *developing and attacking* strategies.

Their key strategies are listed below:

Products

- Package products (ball valves with filters).
- Design new ball valve.
- Design replacement for 'type S' filters.

Pricing

- Additional discount will be offered for online purchases to encourage use of our online shop.
- Penetration policy will be adopted with packages since these will help us to sell more valves.
- Penetration policy will be adopted on 'type K' filters since these generate a large proportion of replacement cartridges.

Promotion

- Change salesforce organisation.
- Recruit additional sales personnel.
- Restructure sales management.
- Increase advertising.
- Increase exhibition coverage.
- Use mailshots/e-mailshots.
- Add 'web analytics' for e-marketing.
- Update and expand website.

Distribution

- Change distribution.
- Appoint distributor sales manager.
- Increase own sales coverage.
- Expand online shop.

Exercise

Now list the key strategies for your marketing plan.
Our key strategies are:

Products

_____

_____

_____

Price

_____

_____

_____

Promotion

_____

_____

_____

Distribution

_____

_____

_____

Schedule of what/where/how

This is the master schedule showing the programme for the implementation of the action plans. Each action plan would be listed either in the master schedule or in a sub-schedule for the functions of product, pricing, promotion or distribution. These schedules indicate to each department and to each member of staff their responsibilities and the timetable for carrying them out. They should take the form of bar charts. An example from the marketing plan of The Equipment Manufacturing Company is shown in Figure 5.6.

The detailed action plans would not be included in the main

MASTER SCHEDULE		
Area: UK *Year:* 20X6		
Month 1 2 3 4 5 6 7 8 9 10 11 12	**Responsibility**	
Action plan	Dept	Person
Restructure	Executive	RLT
E-mail shot	Marketing	AJK
Advertising	Marketing	AJK
Exhibitions	Marketing	AJK
Pricing	Sales	EGM
Distribution	Marketing	AJK
Market analysis	Marketing	AJK
Product design	Engineering	TRG
Expand website	IT	JAT

Figure 5.6   Master schedule for UK plan

body of the marketing plan, but could be included in an appendix.

Exercise

Prepare a master schedule for your own plan:

_____

_____

_____

Sales promotion

Under this heading you should detail your advertising and promotions plan. This includes your personnel requirements as well as advertising and sales promotion.

You should define the mix of distribution channels that you will be using and the structure of your sales organisation, including any changes that you intend to make as part of your plan. You should include a list of existing and additional sales personnel as well as an organisation chart for the sales department. The charts can be included as an appendix to the main plan. Examples of the sales organisation charts and the presentation of existing and additional personnel used by The Equipment Manufacturing Company in its plan were given in Chapter 4 in Figures 4.3, 4.4 and 4.5.

You should include the details and costs of your advertising and sales promotion campaigns. A detailed advertising and promotions schedule for the next 12 months should be included as an appendix.

Budgets and the profit and loss account

The minimum information that should be included is the total cost of implementing the plan. This needs to confirm that the return in increased contribution and profit justifies the expenditure in the action plans and the advertising and promotion plan. The budgeted extra costs will have an effect on the company profit and loss account. The additional sales projected by the plan and the extra costs involved must be presented in the written plan in a way that shows the extra contribution that the plan will make to company profits. The figures should be presented as shown in Table 4.3. They can also be presented as a complete profit and loss account for the area and products of the plan.

A complete profit and loss account for The Equipment Manufacturing Company for its UK sales operations with increased sales is shown in Table 5.5.

Table 5.5   Profit and loss account for UK operations

	20X6 £K	20X7 £K	20X8 £K
Invoiced sales	2,260	2,576	2,937
Cost of sales	1,356	1,507	1,674
Gross profit	904	1,069	1,263
Sales & Marketing costs			
Salaries	239.8	249.4	259.4
Recruitment	9.1	3.2	3.4
Travel/entertaining	37.9	39.4	41.0
Car costs	20.4	21.2	22.0
Advertising	21.3	22.2	23.0
Exhibitions	38.3	11.0	26.4
Literature	15.3	36.0	31.7
Sundry items	10.3	10.7	11.1
Total sales costs	392.4	393.1	418.0
Administration costs	159.0	166.4	174.1
Data processing costs	32.0	33.3	34.6
Distribution costs	60.0	65.0	70.0
Total operating expenses	643.4	657.8	696.7
Operating profit	260.6	411.2	566.3

Exercise

Prepare a profit and loss account for your plan:

Controls and update procedures

It is important to have a suitable monitoring and control system to measure performance in achieving the objectives of the marketing plan and to recommend corrective action where necessary. This monitoring and control system should be included in the written plan.

The control process involves:

- *Establishing standards* – these would relate to the budgeted sales and costs and the timescales for the implementation of the action plans.
- *Measuring performance* – this would compare actual performance against the standards.
- *Proposing measures to correct deviations from the standard* – by detailing corrective procedures to be implemented if the variation from standard exceeds certain limits. These limits should be defined in the written plan.

The control system will operate on the people who are responsible for implementing the plan rather than on the schedules and costs themselves. It should be easy to operate and should allow reasonable variations from the standards before it comes into action.

The controls should be detailed in the written plan. The Equipment Manufacturing Company has included the following controls in its plan:

There will be quarterly marketing plan meetings. A summary of costs against budget and actual progress against the schedules will be prepared for these meetings. A report on the implementation of the action plans will also be presented at these meetings.

Your marketing plan is not set in stone. As you implement it you will find that economic conditions may change, certain strategies may not be as effective as you thought and there may be delays in the implementation of some action plans. Conversely the plan may prove more successful than you anticipated and order intake levels expected in two years may be achieved in one year.

Because of this, an update procedure should be included in the written plan. This may simply state 'This plan is to be revised every 12 months.' Certainly all marketing plans should be updated on an annual basis.

Exercise

State the controls and update procedures for your plan:

_____

_____

_____

Summary

The written plan is the document that will transmit the detail of the plan to those who will implement it. It should only contain the key information that needs to be communicated. Excessive and irrelevant detail should be excluded.

The information should be presented in a logical order. It should include an introduction giving the background to the plan, the reasons for its preparation and its purposes and uses. It should also include an executive summary which should present the key points of the plan in a clear and concise form.

The assumptions on which the plan is based should be clearly stated and information on sales, strategic markets, key products and key sales areas should be presented. The marketing objectives are the aims of the plan and the strategies explain how these objectives will be achieved. The master schedule is the programme for implementation of the action plans.

The advertising and promotions plan includes the personnel requirements as well as advertising and sales promotion. The total cost of implementing the plan and its justification must be shown.

The plan needs to include a suitable control system to measure performance in achieving its objectives and to recommend corrective action where necessary.

6

Presenting the plan, follow-up and revision

You should now have completed your plan. You can compare it with the final version of the UK marketing plan for The Equipment Manufacturing Company which is shown at the end of this book.

Your task is not over when the written plan is complete. It must then be communicated – both to those who must agree to its implementation and to those who will implement it. If a plan is not properly communicated, it will fail. It will fail to be approved and it will fail in its implementation. So it is important to present the plan and to make sure that everyone understands it, rather than just sending a copy by e-mail. If you have consulted properly during the preparation of the plan, it will be 'our plan' rather than 'my plan'. Remember that the contributors to the plan will be better motivated to help implement it if they have been involved in the planning process.

It can be a mistake to distribute the complete plan too widely – the UK sales manager does not need all of the detail of plans for export territories and likewise the export sales manager does not need all of the UK plan. A marketing plan is a sensitive and confidential document that would be of considerable interest to competitors and could be damaging in the wrong hands. Personnel do move on and they take information with them. Copies would obviously need to be supplied to senior executives of your company, but the plan should also be distributed to the heads of department such as accounts, R & D and manufacturing who would be affected by or involved in its implementation.

Presenting the plan

Presentation of the plan needs to be even more clear and concise than the written document itself. You may only have an hour – or even less – to present a plan that has taken many months to prepare.

Nowadays, everyone uses overhead presentations, but some types of presentation package make a greater impact than others. I favour the use of the Microsoft Office software package with the PowerPoint presentation programme. PowerPoint is extremely powerful and if used properly it can make a tremendous impression. The slides are prepared on a PC. They can be used as a presentation package on the PC or they can be printed off onto overhead transparencies. The package itself is in colour – so use it! If you prepare the presentation on overhead transparencies they can be printed in colour.

However, PowerPoint really comes into its own if you make the presentation from a PC. This can be done in a number of ways:

- **You can use a PC with a reasonably large screen.**
- **You can connect a laptop to a larger PC screen.**
- **You can connect your PC/laptop directly to a projector.**

But you can also make your presentation at the same time to company members who are in other offices, other countries or working from home. If you have a videoconference system in your company, you can use this to talk with people in other offices and also run the PowerPoint presentation on a PC in their office at the same time as you make the presentation in your own office (videoconferencing facilities can also be rented in large hotels or business centres). Alternatively, you can use a 'web conference' and talk to people in other offices or working from home. A 'web conference' uses a facility available from a number of companies that specialize in this method of communication. All the people taking part are given website details and a password. They can then log onto the website shortly before the web conference is scheduled. At the same time they call a conference call phone number that has been provided. All of the people who have logged into the web conference can talk on the conference call and they all see the same information on their PC. So the PowerPoint presentation can be run and the presentation and discussion takes place on the telephone conference call.

Whatever means you use to make the presentation, it is important that all present can easily read all of the slides. This means that you should use large font sizes on your slides and not try to cram too much writing onto one slide. If you are making the presentation before an audience, you should use a large screen and make sure that the projector is powerful enough for the presentation to be seen clearly without the need to darken the room.

It looks more professional if you prepare a template with your company name and logo (if you have one) on it. A template can be prepared to be used with the whole presentation. In PowerPoint, headings such as the plan's title and your company name and logo can be added to the slide master. Figure 6.1 shows the PowerPoint template that The Equipment Manufacturing Company has prepared for use in its presentation. The letters 'EMC Ltd' and the seal at the bottom of the slide template are the company's housemark and corporate logo and are used on all company presentations. The heading 'marketing plan 20X6' is used just for this presentation.

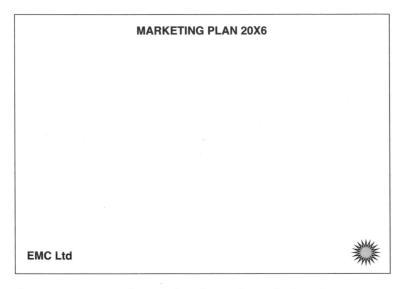

Figure 6.1   PowerPoint template for use in marketing plan presentation

A background colour could also be applied.

The beauty of using PowerPoint is that you can prepare slides from scratch, or you can import files from Word or Excel. These can be text, tables or graphics. PowerPoint also includes a full range of graphic images called 'Clipart'. These include maps of countries and continents, images of computers, and little cartoon people. You can also import digital photographs. The use of some of these items in the right places will brighten up any presentation. But do not overdo it!

Other techniques that can be used include bringing in bullet points one-by-one on a slide. This will prevent your audience from trying to read the whole slide instead of listening to your presentation. Sound and video can also be used, but again they should be used in moderation or they will detract from the presentation, rather than support it.

Figures 6.2–6.8 are some examples of a few of the PowerPoint slides that The Equipment Manufacturing Company has prepared for the presentation of its marketing plan.

Figure 6.2 Introduction slide

Figure 6.3 Sales areas

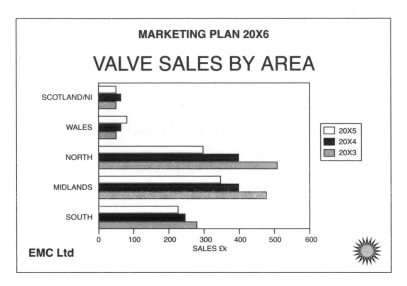

Figure 6.4   Valve sales by area

Figure 6.5   Objectives

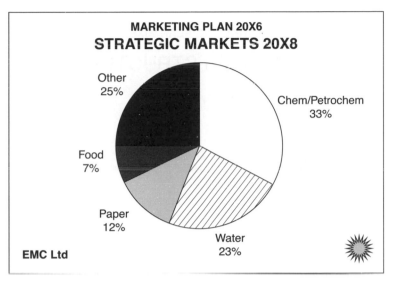

Figure 6.6   Strategic markets 20X8

Figure 6.7   Strategies

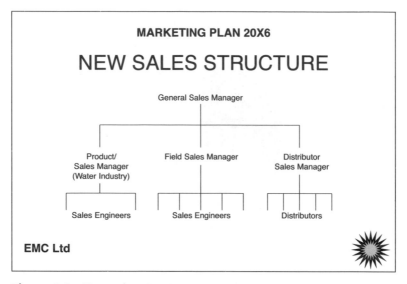

Figure 6.8   New sales structure

Follow-up and revision

Having written and presented your plan, now implement it, and you will start to see results. Your controls and update procedures will enable you to monitor progress and make changes.

Most companies use their marketing plans as a basis for the annual budgeting process. As you proceed with your plan, you can list the things that have gone well over the previous year and also the things that have gone badly. You should list your key tasks and give a status report on those that have been completed and those that have not.

And so the iterative process continues: from marketing plan to budget – from budget to update/revision of marketing plan – and on to the next budget. This iterative procedure can be simplified if you set up basic formats for both your marketing plans and budgets on your PC. The layout of the marketing plan that I have shown you in this book lends itself to being set up as a blank format in Word, with blank spreadsheets in Excel. If you lay it out with numbered pages, you can enforce a discipline with others in your company so that a common company standard is used for marketing plans and budgets and the presentation of both. This will also make it easier for those with less training or experience in marketing planning than you, to prepare the plans that are necessary for their part of the business.

The biggest advantage of a common format is that any individual plan can easily be incorporated into the overall company marketing plan, and sets of figures can be added together in interlinked spreadsheets.

Conclusion

The experience that you have gained in following the procedures in this book will make your company's marketing planning easier and more professional in the future. Practice makes better, but not perfect, and each time the marketing planning process is followed through, the results will improve.

With the best planning in the world, markets are still affected by forces outside your control, but with a proper marketing plan and an understanding of the marketing planning process you can adapt to the changing conditions in which we live.

Appendix

MARKETING PLAN

for

THE UK MARKET

20X6

THE EQUIPMENT MANUFACTURING COMPANY LTD

3rd February 20X6

Contents

Section

1. Introduction

2. Executive summary

3. Situation analysis – assumptions
                        – sales (history/budget)
                        – strategic markets
                        – key products
                        – key sales areas

4. Marketing objectives

5. Marketing strategies

6. Schedules

7. Sales promotion

8. Budgets and profit and loss account

9. Controls and update procedures

   Appendices

1. Introduction

UK sales have stagnated in recent years. The company has always sold a reasonable amount of product into the water industry, but it has never been a key activity area. Because of this, we knew little of the industry or of the potential in it for our product. With the enforcement of EU directives for water treatment and sewage disposal, the industry is now again carrying out a major capital improvement programme. It was therefore felt by the sales and marketing director that we needed to analyse our position in the market and prepare for growth to take advantage of the increased level of spending by the industry.

2. Executive summary

Although our total sales in the UK market have fallen, sales of filters have tripled in the last three years. The increase in filter sales has been mainly into the water industry. Our problem area has been ball valves where we only have a 10 per cent market share, with low sales in the water industry. We currently have market shares in the water industry of 10 per cent for filters and 5 per cent for valves. We believe that if economic conditions remain stable, we will be able to gain market share in this expanding market. Also, the packaging of our filters and valves together will give us a competitive advantage.

The objective of this plan is to achieve 10 per cent growth in UK sales in real terms over the next three years, doubling our water industry market share for filters to 20 per cent and doubling our market share for ball valves to 10 per cent of the projected market in 20X8. In doing so, we intend to increase UK overall gross margins from 39 per cent to 43 per cent by 20X8. This plan details how this can be achieved with an investment in personnel and resources, but without any major additional investment in plant and machinery.

3. Situation analysis

3.1 Assumptions

- Inflation will remain at 3 per cent in 20X6, rising to 4 per cent in 20X7 and 20X8.
- Company wage increases will not exceed inflation over the next three years.
- The pound sterling will not strengthen against either the euro or US$ during the timescale of the plan.
- There will be no delay in the timescale for the UK water industry to implement the EU directives on drinking water and effluent.

3.2 Sales (history/budget)

Sales projection for the UK

THE EQUIPMENT MANUFACTURING COMPANY
SALES FIGURES (Historical and Forecast)

Sales Area:	UK					
	◄——— Actual ———►			◄——— Forecast ———►		
Year (all values in £k)	20X3	20X4	20X5	20X6	20X7	20X8
Filters	200	450	600	750	900	1,050
Valves	1,400	1,200	1,000	1,060	1,151	1,287
Components	300	350	400	450	525	600
Total	1,900	2,000	2,000	2,260	2,576	2,937

Refer to appendix 1.01–1.06 inclusive for details of sales and orders for the period 20X3 to 20X5 inclusive and for the sales and order budgets for 20X6 to 20X8 inclusive.

3.3 Strategic markets

Our strategic markets are chemicals/petrochemicals, water, paper and food. Sales in these markets for 20X5 and forecasts for 20X8 are given below:

Ball valves

UK SALES – STRATEGIC MARKETS				
Product: Ball valves	Actual – 20X5		Forecast – 20X8	
Industry	£k	%	£k	%
Chem/Petrochem	360	36	430	33
Water	150	15	300	23
Paper	120	12	150	12
Food	80	8	90	7
Other	290	29	317	25
Total	1,000	100	1,287	100

Filters and components

UK SALES – STRATEGIC MARKETS				
Product: Filters & components	Actual – 20X5		Forecast – 20X8	
Industry	£k	%	£k	%
Chem/Petrochem	200	20	250	15
Water	400	40	900	55
Paper	150	15	220	13
Other	250	25	280	17
Total	1,000	100	1,650	100

Chemical/petrochemical industry

The chemical/petrochemical industry is our biggest market worldwide. In the UK it accounts for more than 25 per cent of our total sales. Although it is a major source of revenue, the market has been hit hard by the move in refining capacity and heavy chemicals production out of high cost areas like Europe to the Far East. We will do well to hold our own in this industry in the UK over the next few years.

Water industry

Sales in the water industry already account for 28 per cent of our UK business. This is the fastest growing sector of our business. The industry is carrying out a major capital investment programme to comply with EU directives for water treatment and sewage disposal. We expect to be able to take advantage of the increased level of spending in the industry.

Paper industry

The paper industry is slowly coming out of recession. Wood pulp prices have risen significantly in recent years and with the growth in the demand for coated paper we expect to see some increase in our valve and filter business. However, growth in the UK market will be slow.

Food industry

Our sales into the food industry are declining. They currently only account for 6 per cent of our UK sales. Competition from stainless steel ball valve suppliers in the Far East is intense and increasing.

Strategic customers

From the 20X5 sales analysis, a list was produced of our major customers. This list (shown in appendix 3.01) contains our top 40 customers in terms of turnover and represents 20 per cent of the customer base and 80 per cent of total UK sales.

Because of the small customer base, ie only 806 accounts in 20X5 and a large amount of business coming from a small number of customers, it is important that our customer base is expanded and developed.

3.4 Key products

The portfolio matrix for our range of products is shown below.

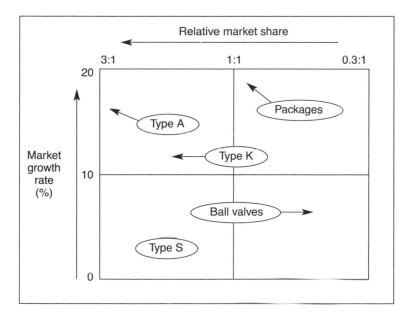

Ball valves

Our ball valve product is nearing the end of its useful life. We intend to carry out a customer/competitor survey over the next six months to define the market requirements for a new product. The development of the new product will take at least 18 months. In the meantime, we will continue to develop sales of the product as a component in our filter packages for the water industry.

Filters

The 'type S' filters have reached the 'saturation' stage of their life cycle, 'type A' filters are at the 'mature' stage of development and the 'type K' filters and packages are in a stage of rapid growth. We expect this to continue.

3.5   Key sales areas

THE EQUIPMENT MANUFACTURING COMPANY
SALES FIGURES (Historical and Forecast)

Sales Area: UK

Product: Ball valves

Year	← Actual →			← Forecast →		
(all values in £k)	20X3	20X4	20X5	20X6	20X7	20X8
South	295	250	230	240	250	260
Midlands	485	415	360	370	390	420
North	525	420	300	325	351	422
Wales	45	55	60	65	70	75
Scotland/NI	50	60	50	70	90	110
Total	1,400	1,200	1,000	1,070	1,151	1,287

THE EQUIPMENT MANUFACTURING COMPANY
SALES FIGURES (Historical and Forecast)

Sales Area: UK

Product: Filters and components

Year	← Actual →			← Forecast →		
(all values in £k)	20X3	20X4	20X5	20X6	20X7	20X8
South	120	252	350	445	565	655
Midlands	164	248	298	348	387	435
North	182	245	277	308	345	395
Wales	20	30	39	51	65	85
Scotland/NI	14	25	36	48	63	80
Total	500	800	1,000	1,200	1,425	1,650

Sales of our established products have traditionally been in the Midlands and the north of England, particularly in the chemical industry. The sales of our filters and components are mainly aimed at the water industry, which covers the whole country. We are particularly strong in the water industry in the south of England with Thames, Southern and Wessex Water. We expect this rapid growth to continue now that we have signed a framework agreement with Thames Water.

The valve business in the Midlands and the north of England has been particularly hard hit by the recession. We expect some improvement now with this product in these areas, but because of plant closures we will not reach the levels of sales that we have achieved in the past.

4. Marketing objectives

- To increase UK sales by 10 per cent per year in real terms for the next three years.
- To double ball valve sales to the water industry within three years.
- To increase sales of packages to 50 units within three years.
- To double market share for filters in the water industry by 20X8.
- To double distributor sales in Scotland and NI by 20X8.
- To increase overall gross margins from 39 per cent to 43 per cent by 20X8.

5. Marketing strategies

Products

- Package products (ball valves with filters).
- Design new ball valve.
- Design replacement for 'type S' filters.

Pricing

- Additional discount will be offered for online purchases to encourage use of our online shop.
- Penetration policy will be adopted with packages since these will help us to sell more valves.
- Penetration policy will be adopted on 'type K' filters since these generate a large proportion of replacement cartridges.

Promotion
- Change salesforce organisation.
- Recruit additional sales personnel.
- Restructure sales management.
- Increase advertising.
- Increase exhibition coverage.
- Use mailshots/e-mailshots.
- Update and expand website.
- Add 'web analytics' for e-marketing.

Distribution

- Change distribution.
- Appoint distributor sales manager.
- Increase own sales coverage.
- Expand online shop.

6. Schedules

Master schedule for UK plan

MASTER SCHEDULE			
Area: UK *Year:* 20X6			
Month	1 2 3 4 5 6 7 8 9 10 11 12	**Responsibility**	
Action plan		Dept	Person
Restructure	⟶	Executive	RLT
E-mail shot	⟶	Marketing	AJK
Advertising	⟶	Marketing	AJK
Exhibitions	⟶	Marketing	AJK
Pricing	⟶	Sales	EGM
Distribution	⟶	Marketing	AJK
Market analysis	⟶	Marketing	AJK
Product design	⟶	Engineering	TRG
Expand website	⟶	IT	JAT

The master schedule shown above is for 20X6. Provisional
schedules for 20X7 and 20X8 are included together with the
individual action plans in appendices 6 and 7.

7. Sales promotion

Our sales of valves are concentrated in the Midlands and the
north of England, where we have good distribution – particularly
through Chemserv in Manchester. We will evaluate our
distribution in this area and consider whether it is viable to
purchase Chemserv as a sales/distribution centre for the north.
Our sales in Wales, Scotland and Northern Ireland are minimal.
The distributors in these areas should be evaluated and possibly
replaced.

Our existing sales structure is shown below:

With this structure, the sales engineers are selling to large key accounts and contracting companies and the UK sales manager is running the salesforce and distribution. This structure lacks focus and we are proposing to change it to the structure shown below.

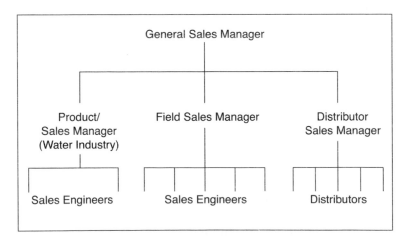

The present UK sales manager will become the field sales manager and we will promote the sales engineer who is our water industry expert to the position of water industry manager. We need to recruit three new people – a general sales manager, a distributor sales manager and a sales engineer.

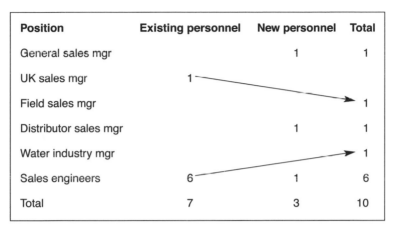

Position	Existing personnel	New personnel	Total
General sales mgr		1	1
UK sales mgr	1		
Field sales mgr			1
Distributor sales mgr		1	1
Water industry mgr			1
Sales engineers	6	1	6
Total	7	3	10

Our main advertising expenditure will be targeted at the water industry. We will also continue our normal advertising/insertions in industry buyers' guides and yearbooks. We will carry out some targeted mail/e-mailshots and expand our website to include 'web analytics' for e-marketing. As well as taking part in The Pump and Valve Exhibition each year as usual, we will take part in the International Water Exhibition in November 20X6 (this exhibition only takes place every three years). Our advertising schedule for 20X6 is shown below.

ADVERTISING

Application: Water Industry   Year: 20X6

MEDIA	No	Rate per insertion £	Total cost £	J	F	M	A	M	J	J	A	S	O	N	D
Water and Waste Treatment	2	1,800	3,600				X					X			
Water Services	2	1,500	3,000						X				X		
Water Bulletin	3	800	2,400			X				X		X			
Water products. com	I	2,000	2,000	X	X	X	X	X	X	X	X	X	X	X	X
TOTAL COST			11,000												

---

8. Budgets and profit and loss account

Operating expenses for the UK operation will increase to fund the additional personnel and sales promotion costs of implementing this plan. The detailed operating expenses budget is shown below.

OPERATING EXPENSES BUDGET FOR 20X6
Department: UK Sales

Item	20X5 expenses	Inflation		Growth	Other	20X6
	£k	%	£k	£k	£k	£k
Salaries	160	3	4.8	75.0		239.8
Recruitment	3	3	0.1	6.0		9.1
Travel/entertaining	30	3	0.9	7.0		37.9
Car costs	14	3	0.4	6.0		20.4
Advertising	10	3	0.3	11.0		21.3
Exhibitions	10	3	0.3		28.0	38.3
Literature	10	3	0.3		5.0	15.3
Sundry items	10	3	0.3			10.3
Total	247	3	7.4	105.0	33.0	392.4

In subsequent years, we will not have such high exhibition costs and the recruitment costs will only occur in the first year. There will be increased costs for literature in years two and three when the new valve and filter products are launched.

The overall effect of the plan is to reduce profits in the first year. They will rapidly recover as our volume growth accelerates in the second and third years. The revised profit and loss account for our UK operations is shown on the next page.

	20X6 £k	20X7 £k	20X8 £k
Invoiced sales	2,260	2,576	2,937
Cost of sales	1,356	1,507	1,674
Gross profit	904	1,069	1,263
Sales & Marketing costs			
Salaries	239.8	249.4	259.4
Recruitment	9.1	3.2	3.4
Travel/entertaining	37.9	39.4	41.0
Car costs	20.4	21.2	22.0
Advertising	21.3	22.2	23.0
Exhibitions	38.3	11.0	26.4
Literature	15.3	36.0	31.7
Sundry items	10.3	10.7	11.1
Total sales costs	392.4	393.1	418.0
Administration costs	159.0	166.4	174.1
Data processing costs	32.0	33.3	34.6
Distribution costs	60.0	65.0	70.0
Total operating expenses (relating to plan)	643.4	657.8	696.7
Operating profit	260.6	411.2	566.3

9. Controls and update procedures

There will be quarterly marketing plan meetings. A summary of costs against budget and actual progress against the schedules will be prepared for these meetings. A report on the implementation of the action plans will also be presented at these meetings.

This plan is to be revised every 12 months.

Appendices

I have not included all the appendices, but a list of them is shown below:

Appendix 1.01 to 1.06   Sales History & Budgets
Appendix 2.01 to 2.02   Unit Sales Analysis
Appendix 3.01   Major Customers
Appendix 4.01   Industry Sector Analysis
Appendix 5.01   Sales Territory Map
Appendix 6.01 to 6.02   Schedules
Appendix 7.01 to 7.08   Action Plans
Appendix 8.01 to 8.10   SWOT Analyses
Appendix 9.01 to 9.04   Competitor Analysis

Creating Success series

The above titles are available from all good bookshops.
For further information on these and other Kogan Page titles, or
to order online, visit the Kogan Page website at
www.koganpage.com

The sharpest minds need the finest advice. **Kogan Page** creates success.

www.koganpage.com